PSYCHIC PETS
Supernatural True Stories of Paranormal Animals

PSYCHIC PETS

Supernatural True Stories of Paranormal Animals

JOHN SUTTON

BEYOND WORDS Publishing INC

Beyond Words Publishing, Inc.
20827 NW Cornell Road
Hillsboro, Oregon 97124
503-531-8700/1-800-284-9673

For a free catalog of other titles by Beyond Words Publishing, Inc.,
please write to us at the address above or call our toll-free number.

First published in Great Britain in 1997
Bloomsbury Publishing Plc, 38 Soho Square, London W1V 5DF

Text design by AB3
Printed and bound in Great Britain by
Clays Ltd, St Ives plc
Distributed to the book trade by Publishers Group West

Library of Congress Catalog Card Number: 97-77586

PHOTOGRAPHY CREDITS
ASTROLOGY FOR PETS: Trevor Roberts of Reed Publications.
THE EXORCIST: Les Gibbon Photography.
THE SHOWJUMPING HORSE-WHISPERERS: Courtesy of Lynne Bowen.

CONTENTS

Welcome to Psychic Pets!   7

What are psychic powers?   10

TEST YOUR PET'S PSYCHIC POWERS: TEST 1
Does it know when you're coming home?   11

The dog that opened the invisible door   13

Cuddles the life-saving cat   18

Myths and legends of supernatural dogs   21

Holly the collie that saw spirits   26

Sam's guardian angel   30

TEST YOUR PET'S PSYCHIC POWERS: TEST 2
Are you in telepathic communication
with your pet?   34

How to develop your pet's telepathic powers   37

Sutty dog and Dulcie Jane   41

The dog that died of a broken heart   44

The psychic pet consultant   47

The show-jumping horse whisperers   52

TEST YOUR PET'S PSYCHIC POWERS: TEST 3
Can your pet see ghosts?   56

The dog that played with ghosts   65

Shandy the psychic Labrador   70

Myths and legends of supernatural cats   72

The curse of Tooty   76

Gypsy the singing cat   81

TEST YOUR PET'S PSYCHIC POWERS: TEST 4
Is your pet clairvoyant?   87

Finn McCoull and Rory, the teleporting pets   91

The exorcist   95

Lucifer the boss cat   99

Astrology for pets   104

The Halloween cat   110

The amazing homing dog   114

Tilley and Bud: A friend from beyond the grave 118

Your psychic personality assessment   121

WELCOME TO PSYCHIC PETS!

My name is John Sutton and as the author of this strange and often weird book I want to assure all readers that I believe the stories within it to be the truth. In my research I have met and interviewed many people and their psychic pets. From a supernatural Halloween cat found on a haunted hill, to a father and daughter showjumping team that can whisper to horses, I have listened to and recorded their often uncanny stories.

You, dear reader, may believe these stories or not, but I feel certain that *Psychic Pets* will make you wonder.

Childhood visions

Before we proceed, let me first tell you a little about myself and the paranormal phenomena that I believe in. Throughout my life—I am now forty-seven years of age—I have experienced odd and often supernatural happenings. As a child, I could see clairvoyant visions of distant lands. Alone in my room I would look at the flowered wallpaper next to my bed and see such things as the creation of the pyramids in ancient Egypt. But as I grew older, these visions ceased. I was programmed into being a 'normal' person living in a material world.

The process starts early. When I was little, I told my parents about what I could 'see' and they told me it was crazy. I trusted them absolutely, they must know best, so I denied the evidence of my sixth sense and gradually it vanished. I was filtering out the psychic information and replacing it with material facts based on accepted science. I grew into a 'normal' person as I was required to do by the society into which I was born. As we all know, 'normal' people do not have clairvoyant psychic sight, do they?

I see a ghost

As a man, I once again began to experience psychic phenomena. My dear father, Frank Sutton, who had been a police detective, returned to see me some months after his death. I saw him sitting in a chair inside my home, a home he had never visited. As I looked into his half-smiling eyes I knew he could not be there, at least not physically. Yet I spoke to him. 'What are you doing here, Dad?' I asked. But in that instant he was gone. He had disappeared into thin air, leaving only his memory behind. I am certain he returned to let me know that all those years before he had been wrong and there is a psychic fourth dimension that exists beyond this physical world.

The psychic world

From that day on I have never doubted that life is eternal, that ghosts exist, that there are more things in this weird and wonderful world than we can even begin to understand. I have continued to break down the mental filters imposed by my social programming. Since the day my father came back, my experiences of the paranormal have forced me to accept that psychic powers exist.

Today I am the feature editor of the journal *Psychic World*, which deals with spiritual and often supernatural occurrences. I have met and worked with many psychics and witnessed their gifts.

It is my belief that there are those among us who can 'see' with psychic powers, but they have to overcome the problem of their social programming. Pets and animals have no such difficulty. They are, I believe, totally natural creatures who are able to receive information through their sixth sense, see ghosts, glimpse the future, and transport themselves through time and space.

Test it out!

In this book I have brought you many true-life stories of animals that have displayed their psychic powers in various ways. I have spoken with the people who own these pets and they seem to me to be ordinary people telling the truth. However, as the reader, you must decide whether you are convinced by their stories. To better enable you to make up your mind, I have devised a multiple-choice psychic assessment at the end of each strange tale. You are invited to use this to help form a decision on exactly what you think the truth is in the story.

The more adventurous readers may like to test and develop their own pets' psychic powers. There are a number of specially designed tests and score charts to help you do this. You can even take your pet on a ghost hunt!

Feedback

If, having read this book, you think you have a psychic pet of your own, why not tell me about it? Who knows—perhaps you and your pet could be in the next volume of *Psychic Pets*. Write to: John Sutton, Psychic Pets, c/o Beyond Words Publishing, Inc., 20827 N.W. Cornell Road, Suite 500, Hillsboro, Oregon, 97124.

WHAT ARE PSYCHIC POWERS?

Telepathy

The communication of thoughts to people or animals by using only the mind. Telepathic communication does not rely on the normal five senses of touch, taste, hearing, sight and smell.

Teleportation

Transporting oneself in an instant to another place. Teleports (also called apports) are believed to happen through a fourth dimension beyond those accepted by the science of geometry—length, breadth and depth.

Clairvoyance, or psychic sight

Perceiving something by visualisation, forming a thought picture in the mind. This psychic power exists beyond the five accepted senses and enables gifted ones to see ghosts.

Clairaudience

The ability to 'hear' voices conveying information without using any of the accepted five senses. Such voices are often thought to be communications from the spirit world.

Precognition

The gaining of information or knowledge relating to forthcoming events without use of reasoning or any of the accepted five senses.

You decide!

There is no scientific evidence to support the above. These psychic powers may or may not exist in some people and animals. You, the reader, must decide.

TEST YOUR PET'S PSYCHIC POWERS: TEST 1

DOES IT KNOW WHEN YOU'RE COMING HOME?

This test is designed to assess your pet's psychic attunement to you, its owner. It is most likely to work with dogs but well worth trying on cats or birds. It is a three-day test.

When you go to school or out for the day, get a friend or a parent to act as your assistant and watch your pet closely just before the time you have agreed to return. You must vary the time that you arrive home over the three days, to avoid creating a pattern. Ask the assistant to fill in the form on the following page.

Try not to get home later than the time you agreed with your assistant, who may not want to observe your pet closely for an extra half-hour while you're hanging out with your friends.

1) Five minutes before agreed arrival time, did pet seem to become more active?

YES ☐ NO ☐   YES ☐ NO ☐   YES ☐ NO ☐

2) Three minutes before agreed time, did pet move towards the front door or look that way?

YES ☐ NO ☐   YES ☐ NO ☐   YES ☐ NO ☐

3) One minute before arrival time, did pet begin jumping up and down or show other signs of excitement?

YES ☐ NO ☐   YES ☐ NO ☐   YES ☐ NO ☐

4) On arrival, did pet greet owner?

YES ☐ NO ☐   YES ☐ NO ☐   YES ☐ NO ☐

Total your answers: YES ☐   NO ☐

Refer to the table below for your pet's PSYCHIC ASSESSMENT.

YES 9–12	Extremely strong psychic link
YES 5–8	Good psychic link
YES 1–4	Some psychic link but needs development
All NOs	Are you sure your pet is still alive?

THE DOG THAT OPENED THE INVISIBLE DOOR

Pets often seem to know when one of their friends is ill or in need of help. Frequently they will lie close to an injured owner or one of their fellow animals to keep them warm and comfort them. This story is one example.

It begins in the year 1981 in the little town of Kunumurra in Western Australia with a business executive named Riete Camer-Pesci. Since her youngest daughter had left for boarding school, Riete returned each evening from her office to an empty home.

A surprise present

Riete's son Gary, who lived in Perth, was worried that his mother might be lonely. One day he telephoned Riete and told her to go to the airport and collect a surprise present he was sending her.

That present was a purebred German short-haired pointer he called Sam.

At first Riete didn't much like Sam, a skinny thing with a long body and wobbly legs, who needed lots of attention. However, she soon grew fond of her new pet, and the two became inseparable. She would even take Sam with her to the office.

Most summer evenings Riete and her friend Sue, who lived on the other side of town, used to drive out into the bush for picnics. Riete took Sam along and Sue took Ben, her basset hound. All four used to play and swim together in the river Ord, which was a great way of cooling off from the Australian heat. Their friendship continued in this way for five years.

The bite of the brown snake

Then in 1986 Gary, Riete's son, returned from Perth to work in Kunumurra. One hot day in November he set off with Sam in tow to visit a nearby farm. While walking along a dusty path, Sam was bitten by a king brown snake. These snakes are venomous and their bite can be deadly. The poison quickly spread through the dog's body and within minutes he was unconscious. Gary placed Sam's limp form on the passenger seat and drove as fast as he could back home.

When Riete saw her friend Sam collapsed, she nearly fainted. But she pulled herself together and drove Sam to the nearest pharmacy. She wanted to buy some antitoxin against the snake venom, but when she got there, they had none. Riete was close to panic, seeing that life was slipping away from her friend.

From the pharmacy Riete drove to a vet's clinic. There they had some antitoxin, but it was months out of date. They used it anyway, for it was Sam's last chance. The vet injected the dog and handed him back to Riete. Sam was already on death's doorstep.

That night Riete held her pet close in her arms and remembered all the happy days they had shared with Ben and Sue out in the bush. She could hardly hear him breathing and his pulse was very weak. There was nothing further Riete could do for him. Before going to bed, she laid him gently on a blanket on the open veranda outside her bedroom.

A mystery visit

Suddenly Riete was awake. She looked at her bedside clock and it said 4 a.m. Outside on the veranda she could hear something moving. In a rush it all came back to her: Sam was ill. Quickly she climbed out of bed and ran out into the cool night air. There, standing next to Sam and licking his face, was Ben the basset hound.

Riete could hardly believe what she saw, because the house had a secure fence all round it and every door was locked. Ben lived with Sue on the other side of town, a long way off, and each night Sue locked him into his room. Yet here he was, comforting his sick friend.

Riete checked Sam for vital signs. There was a pulse, but it was very faint. She telephoned the vet, who came straight over and put Sam on a saline drip. For days he was on the brink of death. Throughout that time Ben refused to leave Sam's side. He just lay down next to his friend and gently licked his face.

It took over a week of constant care, but Sam lived on. Within a month he was able to return to the river Ord and swim once more with Riete, Sue and his best friend Ben.

A door in time and space?

To this day neither Riete nor Sue can offer a rational explanation of how Ben got on to the veranda that night when his friend needed him so badly. Sue, who had been unaware of Sam's plight, clearly recalls locking Ben into his sleeping quarters inside the laundry room of her home. All the doors to her house were also locked and the premises were enclosed by a wire fence.

When I spoke to Riete, she told me that it was her belief that the love between the two dogs had opened a mysterious door in time and space. Through that door Ben the basset hound had traveled on his mission of mercy.

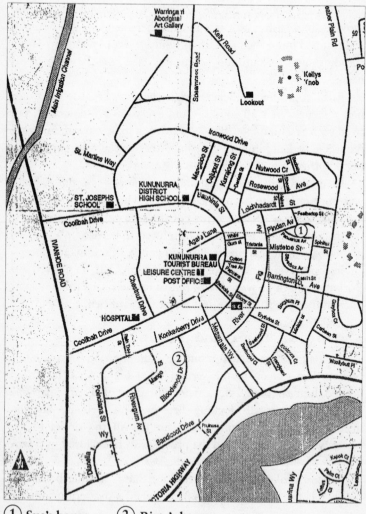

① Sue's house   ② Riete's house

PSYCHIC ASSESSMENT

Q: Can pets tell whether somebody is ill?

a) No, they just like to lie next to another creature for warmth.

b) Yes, they seem to be able to sense this.

c) Yes, even from a distance they know if something is the matter with someone they love.

Q: How do you think Ben the basset knew that Sam was in need of help?

a) He didn't know, but he had got loose that night and came looking for his friend.

b) Ben picked up Sam's cry for help telepathically.

c) Sam's spirit traveled to Ben and asked him to come.

Q: Do you believe that Ben traveled through time and space?

a) No, the very idea is silly.

b) Ben got to Riete's house by jumping the fence.

c) Yes, there is no other explanation.

CUDDLES THE LIFE-SAVING CAT

Dede Summerscales is a happily married woman from the Western Australian town of Kalamunda. Were it not for her cat, her life might have ended many years ago.

The night before the wedding

It was late in the evening of September 8, 1978. Dede was to get married the following day. The excitement of preparing for the wedding had really tired her out and she needed to rest. Dede lived with her parents in a large, old wooden house.

Dede had switched on her electric blanket and the bed was cozy and warm when she got into it. But just as she snuggled down under the covers, she heard her bedroom door being rattled. It sounded as if someone wanted to to get in. Thinking it might be her mother coming to check her wedding dress again, Dede climbed reluctantly out of bed.

When she opened the door, her little cat Cuddles ran in and

jumped up on the bed. Dede was a bit puzzled by this, because Cuddles always slept downstairs. As she watched, the cat crawled underneath the comforter and settled down on top of the electric blanket.

Fire

Back in bed, Dede fell almost instantly into a deep sleep. The heat from the electric blanket soothed her tired body.

It was probably less than a couple of hours later that Dede was forced to wake. Cuddles the cat was licking her face and making a rather odd "Meeooow" sound. As Dede gradually came out of her sleep, she noticed that the room smelled of smoke. Something was definitely burning.

Cuddles the cat continued meowing and scratching at Dede's nightdress. Suddenly Dede became fully awake and she knew what it was: the electric blanket was about to catch fire. She jumped straight out of bed and unplugged it at the main socket on the wall.

Cuddles is a hero

The next morning when Dede's father checked the wires of the blanket, he found that the connection between the electric cord and the blanket had overheated and begun to melt. Had she not switched it off when she did, Dede would have burned in her bed, and probably the entire wooden house would have been destroyed by fire.

Dede told her mother that it was Cuddles the cat who had saved all their lives. Had he not woken Dede up from her deep sleep by licking her face and pawing her cheek and crying, there would have been three funerals and no wedding.

PSYCHIC ASSESSMENT

Q: Why do you think Cuddles banged at Dede's bedroom door?

a) The cat was cold.

b) Cuddles could sense that Dede would be leaving the next day.

c) Cuddles had a psychic precognition of the fire.

Q: Why did Cuddles wake Dede?

a) Cuddles smelled smoke.

b) Cuddles got too hot in the bed and wanted to be let out.

c) The cat was trying to save Dede's life.

MYTHS AND LEGENDS OF SUPERNATURAL DOGS

Humankind's oldest friend is the dog. Originally domesticated more than 14,000 years ago, dogs have been our companions ever since.

The first dogs were really tamed wolves, and all dogs are members of the wolf family. Since humans first trained them to guard the caves they lived in, dogs have been thought to have supernatural powers.

Mythology of dogs

● The ancient Egyptians worshipped a dog-headed god they called Anubis. Many of Egypt's temples were guarded by dogs, who were thought to see evil spirits and frighten them away.

● In Chinese mythology, dogs are also thought to drive away evil spirits. In terms of Yin and Yang, the complementary life forces, dogs are Yang, associated with light and energy.

● In old Arabia, the Saluki dog was believed to be a sacred creature given to the Arab nation by Allah.

● The ancient Greeks had a goddess called Hecate, who was the goddess of witchcraft. Two huge black dogs were her constant companions, and there were numerous sacrifices of dogs made in worship of this evil being.
   In Greek mythology, the gates of hell are guarded by a fifty-headed dog called Cerberus.

● In North America, the Navaho and Karok Indians believed that coyotes, close cousins of the dog, were supernatural creatures.

● One tribe of Native Amerians, the Tinneh, had a creation myth according to which the world was formed out of the pieces of a divine dog that had been torn apart in battle.

● The Iroquois Indians used to sacrifice a white dog at their New Year festival, believing it would take the prayers of their tribe to the happy hunting ground.

● An old Siberian Russian belief is that human souls enter into the bodies of animals on death. The weakest 'go to the dogs'.

● The ancient Syrians believed that dogs were the spiritual brothers of human beings.

● The Islamic religion holds that all dogs are unclean. To call someone a dog is therefore a serious insult.

● The Maori people of New Zealand believe that all dogs have souls which live on after death.

Legendary dogs

Throughout history, people have been telling stories about incredible supernatural dogs. Although dogs in such stories are generally able to both see and hear spirits, they are not understood to enjoy this. A dog sensing a ghost will usually bare its teeth and bark loudly, and the fur at the nape of its neck will stand on end.

A traditional Welsh belief is that death is brought by the ghostly hounds of Annwn. These weird creatures are thought to be seen by real dogs, which howl in terror at the sight of these dreaded beasts.

There are many legends of ghostly black dogs that are thought to be evil. These supernatural creatures are supposed to haunt the sites of gallows, where criminals were hanged. Some believe that the wicked soul of the executed took on the form of a black dog at death. Now these spirits walk the night seeking revenge for their untimely end which they met hanging from the gallows.

Peel Castle on the Isle of Man is supposedly haunted by an evil ghost dog. One night in the early eighteenth century, a guardsman saw what he thought to be a huge black dog lurking round the castle gate. Despite warnings from his fellow soldiers, he set off after the beast. When he returned some few hours later, he was in a terrible state. We shall never know exactly what he saw, because within two days, he was dead. Since then the black dog has been seen many times, but no one dares to follow it.

Elisabeth Device, one of the women accused in the infamous witch trials in England, had a big black dog called Bell. She was alleged to have used this wicked-looking creature as her familiar spirit. According to the testimony of her young daughter Jennet, Elisabeth sent the dog to kill and mutilate two brothers in a nearby town.

In the far north of England, the dark country lanes are, according to legend, haunted by a giant dog they call the Barguest. This enormous doglike creature has saucer eyes and massive jaws. Some say it is waiting for victims.

Dog superstitions

In medieval Britain it was thought that a piece of a dog's tongue hung round the neck could cure people of a form of tuberculosis. This illness was also called the king's evil because another supposed cure was to have a king touch the afflicted person.

One old remedy for illness was to cut a lump of hair from the head of a sick person, place it between two slices of buttered bread and feed it to a dog. The sickness was supposed to be transferred to the unfortunate creature.

It was also believed that the life of a dog is closely linked to that of its owner. When the owner dies, the dog is expected to follow soon after.

Dog history

When the King of England had an official residence at Greenwich, London, his hunting dogs were held in kennels on the opposite side of the river Thames. The site of the kennels is now called the Isle of Dogs.

The dog credited with saving the greatest number of lives in England is Swansea Jack, who, during the 1930s, repeatedly dived into the sea from the docks and helped save as many as twenty-five seamen who had, at various times, fallen in.

In England there is a special award made to outstandingly brave dogs: the Dickin Medal, given by the National Canine Defence League. Heroic American dogs receive the Animal Hero Medal from the American Humane Education Society.

There is a Dog Star in the heavens, Alpha Canis Majoris, usually called Sirius. The days of late July and early August are called the dog days because Sirius is then rising. In the western hemisphere, this is often a time of intense heat which can drive dogs crazy.

HOLLY THE COLLIE THAT SAW GHOSTS

It all began with a family day out that was no different from any other. In the early summer of 1995, Steven Johnson decided to take his wife Carolyn and their sixteen-year-old son Christopher on a day trip. They had almost perfect sunny weather all the way there. Holly, the family dog, had been sniffing the fresh air through the open window of the car as they drove along the country road.

They stopped for a rest at a small town. Holly demanded a walk, so Christopher let her out of the car, and together the family set off strolling along the tree-shaded lane that ran alongside the river. Reaching an old church, they went through the gate to have a look, and strolled along a winding path through the church grounds.

The ghost in the graveyard

In the quiet graveyard of the church, the grey headstones slant at strange angles towards the sky. Just as they were passing a moss-covered grave, Holly suddenly stopped in her tracks and refused to move. Staring upwards into what the Johnson family thought was empty space, she snarled and growled as if facing an enemy.

Steven called Holly to come away, but she refused. Lowering herself to the ground, as collie dogs do, she bared her teeth and barked as if in warning to an unseen presence that stood before her. Christopher and Carolyn looked on in wonder as their pet faced something only she could see. The fur on Holly's back stood up in terror as the dog tried to defend herself against the unknown entity from beyond the grave. Then, fearing for Holly's wellbeing, Christopher bravely ran forward and threw his arms around his pet.

For a moment there was total silence. It seemed that no bird sang, no gentle breeze eased the leaves of the tall trees, and even the rippling waters of the river calmed. Then everything returned to normal. Something had moved between this world and the next, but only Holly knew what that was. Christopher's bravery had saved his pet from further torment: whatever it was that had been there had gone.

Forgetting any idea they had of going into the church, the Johnson family turned round and went back to their car. They were thankful that Holly seemed none the worse for her experience, but it had certainly scared them all.

Old Mr. Smith

An old gentleman called Mr. Smith lived close to the Johnson family on the same street. He was eighty years old but loved to play with Holly, often bringing the collie biscuits and other little treats. He told Carolyn that years ago, when he was a young man, his family had a dog just like Holly. Their friendship lasted many months, with Holly becoming tuned in to the old man. The collie seemed to know several minutes in advance when her special friend was on his way and would sit barking happily at the front door, wagging her tail in anticipation. It was as if Holly could pick up Mr. Smith's vibrations.

A last farewell

It was a dark and stormy night just before Christmas 1995, and all the Johnson family were asleep in their beds. Holly, who had been out playing in the garden most of the day, lay resting in her box downstairs. It was long past midnight when Carolyn heard Holly barking. Quickly she woke Steven, thinking someone might be trying to break in.

Running downstairs, Steven saw Holly wagging her tail and looking up towards the front door. Every now and then she gave a friendly little bark, as if she were welcoming someone—just the way she did when her friend Mr. Smith called.

Steven wondered whether old Mr. Smith was outside, needing help. Quickly he opened the door. Holly ran to the front step, dancing and jumping as she often did when greeting her friend. But there was no one there. The still, dark street was empty, save for the shadows of night and the cold north wind.

The next morning at breakfast Carolyn answered the telephone. It was the next-door neighbor of their friend Mr. Smith. The old man had been taken ill during the night and died in hospital at three o'clock, the exact time Holly had woken the house with her barking.

Carolyn believes that Holly was visited by the departing spirit of the old man, who called in on his way to paradise to say goodbye to Holly, the dog who had been his friend.

PSYCHIC ASSESSMENT

Q: What do you think scared Holly the collie in the graveyard?

a)   The scent of a fox that lived nearby.

b)   The spooky atmosphere and smell of death.

c)   The ghost of someone buried in the graveyard.

Q: What do you think happened when Christopher grabbed hold of Holly?

a)   The dog gave up the hope of a confrontation with the fox.

b)   The dog was comforted.

c)   The ghost returned to its place in the world beyond.

Q: How did Holly know when old Mr. Smith was coming to visit her?

a)   Mr. Smith always came at the same time.

b)   Holly could hear Mr. Smith walking along the street.

c)   The dog had become attuned to the old man and his vibrations.

Q: When Holly started barking at the closed door, what do you think she was expecting?

a)   A stranger.

b)   A visit from her friend Mr. Smith.

c)   A ghost from the world beyond.

SAM'S GUARDIAN ANGEL

The bond of love that exists between a pet and its owner extends beyond the bounds accepted by science. There are incidents that must cause even the most educated sceptic to ask the question, "If spirits do not exist, then how did this happen?" The mysterious case of Sam, a white West Highland terrier, is one of these stories.

Two dog lovers

Sam's owner was Olga Dakin, a spiritualist medium from England. When in 1990 she was taken ill, Sam was looked after by her son Gary. Gary also visited his mother every day in her hospital ward. Olga would always ask about Sam and often sent little presents to him from hospital, especially chocolate dog biscuits, which he loved.

One day a nurse serving on the ward noticed Sam's picture on Olga's bedside locker and remarked how like her own West

Highland terrier he was. They quickly became friends as Olga told the kindly nurse all about her pal and his funny ways.

The nurse would often stop at Olga's bed and have a chat about dogs in general and "Westies" in particular. Those talks cheered Olga very much, but she was a dying woman. The doctors could not save her, and one dark day in late October she passed away. Sam would never again see his friend, or bark joyfully as she opened a packet of his favorite dog biscuits.

A new home for Sam

Gary Dakin, who had been looking after Sam for his mother, now had a problem. He couldn't keep Sam permanently, because he worked all day and felt it would not be fair on the dog to be alone for so long. So he asked an acquaintance called Helen Rooke if she would have Sam. Helen was pleased to accept. She loved West Highland terriers and had always wanted one.

Helen Rooke lives in a very busy and built-up part of the city, but Sam soon settled into his new home. She even gave him chocolate dog biscuits to let him know that he was loved. Then one day, by mistake, someone left the front door open. Sam ran out into the street and got lost.

Lost on the highway

Helen was really worried about the little dog. This was still a strange area to him, and out there in the fast-falling darkness he would never find his way home. Moreover, her house is close to a main road, and she feared he would be killed. In tears she called Gary Dakin to ask for his help. Together they searched throughout the neighborhood but Sam was not to be found.

The highway near her home is one of the most dangerous roads in the city. There are two lanes in each direction where the cars roar along at sixty miles an hour or more. It was along this highway that a young woman was driving home from work when she suddenly felt an irresistible urge to stop.

The good samaritan

Pulling over to the side of the road, she got out of the car. There was no good reason for her to do such a thing. It was a cold, dark night, rain was falling quite heavily and she was already late. But something unseen made her shut the car door and walk towards a clump of bushes growing at the edge of the road.

Underneath these bushes, cowering wet and injured, lay a little white West Highland terrier.

Lifting the dog up, she held it close and gently stroked its head, comforting the poor, lost creature. Around its neck was a collar and a tag with the name "SAM" and a telephone number.

The guardian angel

Helen received the telephone call just before nine that night. She was immensely relieved to learn that her dog was safe. He was slightly hurt, having been hit by a car, but he would be OK. His kind rescuer invited Helen to come over and pick up her dog as soon as she liked. Helen was in her car and on the way in minutes.

Arriving at the stranger's home, Helen couldn't thank her enough. She had been so worried. Sam looked a bit shaken up but, apart from his bruises, he was fine. He'd even made a new friend in his rescuer's dog: a West Highland terrier just like Sam. They had been playing together.

Refusing the offer of a reward for saving Sam, the woman told Helen how she happened to find him. "It was a strange feeling I had—it just came over me, as if something were telling me to stop. I can't really say why I did. I was late for my dinner as it was."

Helen thought about this and jokingly replied, "It must have been his guardian angel coming to his aid. Probably the ghost of Olga, Sam's previous owner."

The other woman looked startled; all the color drained from her face. "Did you say Olga?" she asked, staring at Sam. "There was a patient called Olga on my ward at Tameside General Hospital—I'm a nurse. She used to talk to me about the love she had for her pet dog."

PSYCHIC ASSESSMENT

Q: Why did Sam run away?
a) He wanted to explore his new surroundings.
b) He wanted to return to his old home.
c) He was looking for Olga.

Q: Why do you think the nurse stopped her car and found Sam?
a) Out of the corner of her eye she had seen something moving.
b) The nurse was psychically tuned in to Sam, having seen his picture.
c) The spirit of Olga guided her.

TEST YOUR PET'S PSYCHIC POWERS: TEST 2

ARE YOU IN TELEPATHIC COMMUNICATION WITH YOUR PET?

This series of three tests involves you, your pet and an assistant. It does not have to be the same person each time. The assistant must score each part of this test according to close observation of your pet and yourself. None of the tests will work with fish or any animal that is not allowed to run or fly about the room.

The toy thought test

1) With your pet and the assistant out of the room, hide your pet's favorite toy in a place where it would not normally be.

2) Bring in the assistant and your pet. Maintain complete silence and don't signal to your assistant where you've hidden the toy.

3) Now concentrate your mind on an image of the toy in its new location and try to project this into your pet's mind. Imagine yourself playing with your pet and its toy. Continue this for five full minutes.

Scoring:

Pet fell asleep before five minutes were up.	0
Pet tried to get out of the room.	1
Pet started playing with assistant.	2
Pet ran round the room as if searching, but did not stop at hiding place.	3
Pet sniffed two or three places, including the hiding place.	4
Pet went straight to the location of the toy.	5

The food thought test

1) Leave your assistant and your pet alone in the room where the experiment is to be held.

2) Your assistant should have some of the pet's favorite food (maybe a piece of meat or a dog treat) and show it to the pet.

3) The assistant then hides the piece of food in an unusual place, showing the pet where it is.

4) Next, the assistant takes your pet into another room.

5) You enter the experiment room, concentrating on your pet and its favorite food. In your mind, try to picture your pet going to where the food is. As soon as you think you know or an image of the location flashes into your mind, go and look.

Scoring:

You searched everywhere and couldn't find it.	0
Your mind went blank.	1
You found the food in the place you thought your assistant was most likely to place it.	2
Your mind filled with a picture of yourself and your pet playing on the beach.	3
You could sense your pet trying to communicate with you but you had to look in two or three places to find the food.	4
You went straight to the location of the food.	5

Notes:

* If your pet loves messy food, make sure it is on a dish or a piece of tin foil so that the hiding place doesn't get stained.

* Do not place it on or close to electrical equipment.
* If you can't find it and your assistant forgets where he or she put it so that the food is not discovered until a week later by an irate family member, you have all failed the test.

The walk thought test

1) Sit close to your pet but not touching. The assistant should have a clear view of both you and the animal.
2) In your mind, picture yourself putting a lead on your pet and/or walking out with it. Project this image into your pet's mind by looking at it and concentrating.
3) Continue this for five minutes with constant thoughts of you and your pet walking out and having fun.

Scoring:

Pet fell asleep.	0
Pet licked your face sympathetically.	1
Pet went straight to the place where the food was hidden in the previous experiment.	2
Pet became excited and wanted to play.	3
Pet went to look out of the window.	4
Pet ran to the door or to fetch its leash.	5

Total your score and refer to table below:

10–15	You have a strong telepathic link with your pet.
5–10	You have telepathic potential but need to develop your powers.
0–5	Try again after practicing the development exercise. And tell your assistant to stop giggling.

HOW TO DEVELOP YOUR PET'S TELEPATHIC POWERS

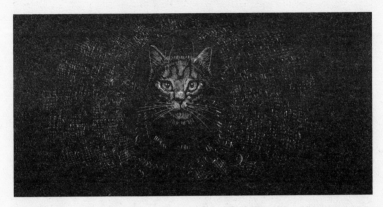

This series of exercises is designed to develop the telepathic link between you and your pet. For the best results you should repeat each exercise daily over a period of at least seven days.

Then, when you think your pet is ready, repeat the relevant tests found elsewhere in this book. They will give you an idea of how your psychic link with your pet is developing. Establishing telepathic communication takes time and patience, so don't blame your pet if it can't read your mind.

To communicate telepathically with an animal, you need to think in pictures and visualize doing something. Each exercise below is broken down into three steps:

a) TALK   b) IMAGE   c) DO.

Exercise 1:   Feeding your pet

For this exercise you will need a bowl of your pet's favorite food.

TALK: At approximately the same time each day, stroke your pet and tell it in your own words that you are going to feed it. Look at your pet as you speak and use just one simple phrase—"It's dinner time" or whatever. Speak clearly and repeat the phrase a number of times while gently stroking your pet.

IMAGE: As you are speaking to your pet, picture in your mind the food you will be giving to it. (Cat food is pretty revolting, but try to see it from the cat's point of view.) Imagine the food in the pet's bowl and try to project this image into your pet's mind as you do so. Stroke your pet softly as you do this—remember, you're tuning in to each other.

DO: After a few minutes of gently stroking and talking to your pet while at the same time imagining the meal, stand up and place the previously prepared bowl of food before your pet. As your pet eats, softly repeat the phrase "It's dinner time" and get the image of your pet eating its food clearly into your mind.

You have now established a simple system of communicating with your pet. (That is, unless your pet spotted the bowl of food at the outset and has been dancing around yowling throughout your attempt to beam thoughts at it.)

Exercise 2: Playing with your pet

For this exercise you will need your pet's favorite toy.

TALK: Gently stroke your pet and talk to it about its favorite toy. Say something like "Nice ball" (there is no need to get clever) and speak with happiness in your voice.

IMAGE: As you speak to your pet, picture the ball or other toy in your mind and imagine playing with it. Keep on repeating the words you decide upon and try to make this sound like fun. Remember you are trying to tune both your minds in to the toy, so picture it clearly. Continue this exercise for at least two to three minutes.

DO: Take the toy and place it before your pet. Repeating the words "Nice ball" or whatever, play with your pet and get a clear image in your mind of your pet enjoying this play. Make it lots of fun and talk to your pet.

(Spending long minutes concentrating on a well-chewed rubber mouse is one of those sacrifices pet owners have to make. Look at it this way: it is better than homework. But if you begin to feel the need to take the rubber mouse to school with you, discontinue this exercise for a time.)

Exercise 3: Walking your pet

This exercise is for dogs and their owners. You will need a leash.

TALK: After your dog has had its main meal, at approximately the same time each day, talk to it about going for a walk. Use a very simple phrase but make sure to include its name; say, "Walk time, Rover!" or "Let's go for a walk, Rover" or whatever you feel happy saying. Ruffle your dog's fur as you speak and sound enthusiastic: this is going to be lots of fun.

IMAGE: As you speak to your dog, picture yourself walking along a familiar street or through a field with your pet by your side. Remember, you are enjoying this imaginary walk. This part of the exercise should last no more than two minutes because by now, if you are doing it correctly, your dog will be jumping about ready to go.

DO: Get your dog's leash and at the same time repeat exactly the words you have chosen—"Walk time, Rover" or whatever. As you fasten the lead, try to take a mental snapshot of yourself doing it. That image will be useful when you repeat this exercise.

Once outside with your dog, stop now and then to stroke its head and repeat the words you have chosen, using its name. This is a fun time, so be happy and send those joyous thoughts to your dog.

Repeat these exercises as instructed to build your pet's psychic powers. Then try Test Two on page 34 again.

SUTTY DOG AND DULCIE JANE

Dulcie Jane was eighteen and still living at home with her parents. Her pet dog Sutty, a Scottish terrier, shared her bedroom. Dulcie had had Sutty since the dog was only a few months old, and over the years they had formed a close psychic link.

The little black terrier even developed the same hesitant way of eating that Dulcie had. Sutty would not just run up and gobble down her food like most hungry dogs. Just like Dulcie, Sutty would stare at whatever meal you placed in front of her and think about it for a while. Sometimes the dog wouldn't touch her dinner at all. This was exactly like Dulcie Jane, a very fussy eater.

In fact, Dulcie and Sutty dog had grown to be so much alike that sometimes Dulcie Jane's mother would call the dog "Dulcie" by mistake. The really odd thing was that the dog would answer to the name and come running up as if her own name had been called.

Sutty dog was always very protective of her Dulcie Jane and

would bark if anyone she didn't like went too close to her. When strangers came to the house, Sutty would start barking and growling. No one could get near Dulcie if Sutty dog was unsure of them; she seemed to able to sense if they were nice people.

The boyfriend test

In the spring of 1994, Dulcie fell in love. His name was Rob. She was very nervous the day she first brought her new boyfriend home to meet her parents. She hoped they would like Rob, but she was aware that Sutty dog might object.

Dulcie had been telling Sutty all about Rob, so she was sure her pet already knew that something was happening. The Scottie always seemed to be in tune with Dulcie—when she was happy, so was Sutty dog. But Dulcie Jane was a little bit worried that her pet might be jealous of Rob. For years they had been best pals and now Sutty would have to share her owner's love with someone else.

Dulcie's steps slowed as she came down the driveway with Rob. As soon as she opened the door, Sutty dog was there. She was making her pretend growling noise and dancing in delight, welcoming Dulcie home. But what about Rob? This was the test. Rob walked into the house and reached down to stroke the dog. For a moment Dulcie held her breath. Then Sutty jumped up and licked Rob's hand, and Dulcie broke out in a big grin.

Dulcie Jane had never seen Sutty do this before. The dog usually took some time to go near a stranger, and she had never met Rob. Her pet really liked Rob at once. She was prancing around happily, just the way she always did for Dulcie Jane. It was as if Sutty knew that this man was her friend too.

When Dulcie saw how well Sutty dog had taken to her boyfriend Rob, she knew he was the one for her.

Dulcie Jane and Rob Dowrick got married in October 1995. Sutty dog couldn't go to the wedding, but she was waiting when they came home to give the happy couple a proper welcome.

From their honeymoon they sent out many postcards. One card was to Sutty dog, and it read: "To our best little pal, Lots of love, Dulcie & Rob."

PSYCHIC ASSESSMENT

Q: What made Dulcie Jane's mother call the dog "Dulcie?"
a) She had been at the cooking sherry.
b) Dulcie's mother was not thinking about what she was saying.
c) Sutty dog reminded her so much of Dulcie that she mixed them up.

Q: Why do you think Sutty dog liked Rob Dowrick?
a) His scent was familiar from the times Dulcie had been out with him.
b) Sutty could sense that Dulcie liked him.
c) Sutty sensed that he was the right man for Dulcie Jane.

THE DOG THAT DIED OF A BROKEN HEART

Mary Wicks lives in the Western Australian town of Armadale. She and her husband Jim had a pet dog, a kelpie (Australian sheepdog) crossbreed they called Chubby. Chubby was Jim's special friend and constant companion for seventeen years.

Surviving fire

In 1991 a fire totally destroyed Mary and Jim's home. Jim was very badly burned. Throughout his recovery, his pet Chubby remained by his side. The dog seemed to know that Jim was sick and he stood guard as if to protect him. As Jim got a little better, he would often sit outside the house, which had been rebuilt, throwing a ball for Chubby to catch. Jim and his pet were together every day, and the dog's steadfast support helped him to recover.

At night Chubby slept outside in his basket on the patio. He was a great watchdog and would bark really loudly if any strangers came near.

Together to the last

Jim Wicks had been suffering from bad headaches for some time. In May 1993 he became seriously ill. Chubby was not normally allowed into the house at night, but on the night of May 18th, Jim woke to hear the dog barking and scratching at the side door. Jim let him in to see what the matter was. Chubby trotted into the bedroom, walked around the bed and sat down next to Jim's side.

All night Chubby sat beside Jim's bed, guarding his master. He could not be persuaded to move.

The next morning Chubby was still there, and he stayed at Jim's side, following him when he got out of bed. At breakfast Mary and her husband talked about Chubby's strange behavior, but neither could explain it.

The next evening at about 8:30, Jim Wicks suffered a stroke and went into a coma. He died on May 21st in a hospital. Chubby, his loyal pet, was left sitting silently on the patio where he had spent countless hours playing with his master.

Over the next few days Chubby's health deteriorated. He seemed to have lost the will to live. On May 27th, 1993 the dog passed away. Mary believes he died of a broken heart.

PSYCHIC ASSESSMENT

Q: Why did Chubby insist on getting into the house?
a) Jim was ill and didn't come out, so Chubby was lonely.
b) Chubby knew that his owner was in need of love and protection.
c) Chubby knew that Jim was going to die.

Q: Did Chubby really die of a broken heart?
a) The dog died of old age—it was seventeen.
b) Chubby was worn out from guarding Jim, and Mary's grief made him feel worse.
c) Yes, the dog lost the will to live when his friend died.

THE PSYCHIC PET CONSULTANT

From her early childhood, Marisa Anderson has been able to perceive the thoughts of other living creatures. Having no language, animals communicate in pictures, using telepathic powers. Being naturally gifted with clairvoyant psychic sight, Marisa tuned in to the animals she met and quickly realized that she was receiving messages from them.

The white horse

When she was a young girl growing up in New York, her family took her to the countryside on a horse-riding holiday. There in a corral stood a beautiful, pure-white mare. Marisa, who loved riding, knew at once that she had to ride it.

The farm owner was shocked when Marisa approached him for permission. This particular horse was very difficult to ride, he warned her: it had a mind of its own.

Standing at the side of the corral, Marisa reached out, placing her hand on the white horse's nose. For a moment she felt it tense; then into her mind came a picture of peace, green fields and gentle streams. The horse wanted to be free, it hated being locked into stables or a corral. Marisa telepathically sent a message to it. She pictured herself on the horse's back riding alongside a river, wind blowing through the trees. Seeming to receive this image, the horse shook its glorious head in delight. From that moment on they were friends.

The farmer stared in amazement as Marisa smoothed the horse's mane. He was even more surprised when Marisa, having helped to put a saddle on its back, climbed on and, with just a little help from the more experienced riders, actually rode the horse.

The hidden chameleon

When Marisa was about nine years old, her family had a pet chameleon lizard called Bonnet. One day Bonnet disappeared and no one could find it. Then suddenly a thought jumped into Marisa's mind; it was as if the lizard were speaking to her. She knew at once where the little creature was. Sure enough, she found it curled up underneath a sofa in the living room.

But Marisa also knew that Bonnet was ill. That was why it was hiding away. The very next day, the chameleon died.

An unusual career

Marisa's mother recognized that her daughter had special powers, but told her that when she grew up her psychic gifts would disappear. However, Marisa's mother was wrong—they didn't. When Marisa left school, she set up her own business as a psychic pet consultant in New York.

When someone's pet becomes ill and needs help, Marisa has the ability to discover what is wrong with it. Soon she got animal patients from various parts of the country, and even many vets agree that Marisa's powers as a psychic pet consultant are beyond doubt.

Sweet William's hot dinner

Sweet William is a red Persian tom cat belonging to Suzanne Finstad, an author and lawyer in Hollywood. One evening she fed her pet, then sixteen years old, some shrimps cooked in a hot cajun-pepper sauce. Later that night, Sweet William became ill.

The next morning Suzanne was so worried that she called her

vet at the Hollywood pet hospital. But her regular vet was not available to see Sweet William. Instead Suzanne took her cat to another vet, who diagnosed liver damage. She admitted Sweet William to the pet hospital and placed him on an intravenous drip.

Suzanne was sure Sweet Wiliam didn't have liver damage, only stomach problems from the shrimp, but the vet said it was definitely his liver and he would have to be injected with fluids daily for the rest of his life. Reluctantly, Suzanne left poor Sweet William in the hospital and drove home.

A long-distance consultation

Back at home, Suzanne looked in her directory of psychic consultants and found the name of Marisa Anderson, the pet specialist. Suzanne called Marisa in New York, and the psychic tuned in her mind to the sick cat. She told Suzanne that Sweet William had eaten something rancid that had caused him to be ill. She even described the color of the cat's vomit. Suzanne was simply amazed.

Over the telephone, Marisa went on to tell Suzanne that Sweet William was lying in the pet hospital dreaming about the happy days when he had spent time in the countryside and run about in the open air. To Suzanne, this was proof of Marisa's psychic powers, because Hollywood is far from pastoral and Marisa could not possibly have known that when Suzanne first got the cat, she was living with her parents in the country.

Marisa told Suzanne not to worry. Marisa would send out healing thoughts to the cat, and he would soon be home. Then Marisa gave her a list of homeopathic remedies to give to her pet once he was out of the hospital. These would help clear his system of any remaining poison.

Recovery

Two days later Suzanne spoke to her usual vet. He told her that the cat was well enough to go home. When Suzanne was picking up Sweet William from the pet hospital, she told her vet about

Marisa and her accurate description of the cat's illness. The vet did not object to her consulting a psychic. He said that in such matters he had an open mind. He agreed with Marisa that the cat had been suffering from a form of food poisoning. Sweet William had a normal liver and the homeopathic remedies Marisa had prescribed would probably help, the vet said.

Today Sweet William is a contented and healthy cat with an owner who believes absolutely that his life was saved by the supernatural healing powers of the psychic pet consultant Marisa Anderson.

The ghost of a white cat

Once, while visiting a friend who is a psychic investigator in New York, Marisa was asked for help. In a block of flats close to her friend's home, the occupants were complaining that their rooms were haunted by a ghost cat. Each night around ten, the spirit of a white cat would walk around the corridors of the building.

Marisa sat down on a chair inside the entrance and waited. As the clock struck ten, she saw a faint white shape materialize in the doorway—the ghost cat. Using clairaudience, tuning her mind in to the cat, she realized that it was looking for its owners, who had lived there when it was alive.

The spirit of the cat told Marisa that it had been happy in the block of flats and wanted to stay but couldn't find its old friends who had moved away. As the thoughts this ghost cat was thinking flashed into Marisa's mind, she knew at once what to do.

Marisa, like all psychics, has spirit guides who help her to help others. For a moment Marisa called upon her guides and pictured the cat walking into the next world with them. In a twinkling, her spirit friends appeared and called the little creature to join them. She watched as the white ghost cat turned and walked away into the world beyond. It has not been seen since.

PSYCHIC ASSESSMENT

Q: When Marisa was a young girl, how did she know she had psychic powers?

a) She had a good imagination and wanted to believe herself to be special.

b) Her empathy with animals enabled her to picture the kind of things they might be thinking.

c) She received telepathic messages from pets and other animals.

Q: How did Marisa find Bonnet the chameleon lizard?

a) She searched everywhere until she found it.

b) She thought of the place where she would go and hide if she were a lizard.

c) The lizard sent out a telepathic message to Marisa.

Q: How did Marisa know about Sweet William's early life?

a) She just guessed.

b) The thought came into her mind.

c) The cat told her by telepathy.

Q: Did Marisa heal Sweet William?

a) The cat would have recovered anyway, it only had indigestion.

b) The treatment in the pet hospital healed the cat.

c) Marisa sent out psychic healing power.

THE SHOW-JUMPING HORSE WHISPERERS

The former Olympic team show-jumper and internationally successful rider David Bowen is a real-life "horse whisperer". David shares his unusual ability with his daughter Sarah, who has also become a top-class show-jumper.

The life-changing accident

The story begins in 1954 in a little village in Lancashire, England. Young David Bowen was playing soldiers with his pals on a building site when he fell into the flooded foundations and nearly drowned.

David was very badly hurt, and his face was tinged blue when they pulled him out of the water. The nurse who saved him thought he was going to die. When he did recover, David had lost the ability to speak properly. All his words jumbled themselves up and no one could understand what he was saying.

For years David went to speech therapy. He hated it. It made him different and as a boy he only wanted to be like his friends.

David discovers his gift

One day David's father, Tom Bowen, took his boy to a big house in the country. The owner had a pony and let David ride it. Almost as soon as he got on the animal's back, he seemed to know what he was doing. Both David's father and the owner were amazed at how well he rode: he was a natural.

Soon afterwards Mr. Bowen offered to pay for David to go to a local riding school called Roocroft's. There David quickly became a star rider. He rode the most difficult pony in the stables and in next to no time at all he was winning ribbons at local competitions. Neither David nor his horse-riding instructors knew just how he did it. Many were puzzled by his habit of riding with long reins. It is totally against everything that a young rider is taught, but for him it works.

From pony-club class to regional competitions, the young David Bowen became famous. He was quickly recognized as being able to make even very difficult horses and ponies do just what he wanted. At the age of sixteen he was winning major national competitions against the very best in the country. As little more than a boy, he jumped at Wembley Stadium in London in the Horse of the Year Show and beat an Olympic silver medalist.

By the time David was twenty-one, he was a full-time professional show-jumper touring the world and winning such events as the Hickstead Derby and the King George V Cup. In 1984 David represented Great Britain at the Los Angeles Olympic Games as a member of the show-jumping team, and they won a silver medal.

David's secret

"When I first sat on a pony as a boy, I sort of knew I could ride," David Bowen told me. "I was at once in tune with it and was almost able to make the pony stop, start, canter or walk by just thinking about it. In my mind I just willed it to do things and the pony did.

"When I started jumping at big events, I found the same thing happening. I would sit on the horse, give it a squeeze with my knees, and off we went. At the fences I just pictured us jumping clear and the horses did it. I don't know why the horses jump well for me, I just seem to be able to whisper to them with my mind and up they go over the fences.

"I think it all started when I was injured as a boy. I wanted to be like everyone else but could hardly speak. It was then my dad encouraged me to ride. I might not have been much of a talker with people, but horses and ponies could understand me— they still can."

The next generation

At the 1996 Hickstead Derby, David's daughter Sarah jumped joint second and was the highest-placed female in the event and, at twenty-two, the youngest.

"I think I'm a lot like my father David," Sarah told me. "Even as a little girl, when I used to ride ponies, I felt able to communicate with them using my mind. I talk to them now, just say 'Good boy' and 'Come on up!' and picture the horse clearing the fences. Horses know when you like them. I just love them, always have, and I know they love me. Exactly what makes them jump for me, I just don't know."

Talking to David and Sarah Bowen, I was deeply impressed with their honest admission that even they were a bit mystified about how they do what they do so well. But to see these two, father and daughter, on top of fine, big horses jumping the fences is to know that something very special is happening. We might call it telepathy, horse whispering, psychic power, just skill or whatever. To me it looked like the incredible power of love.

PSYCHIC ASSESSMENT

Q: When David was a boy, what do you think made him a good rider?
a) Practice and determination.
b) David knew he could ride, so he concentrated on it.
c) David has a telepathic ability to communicate with horses.

Q: Do you think David's injury as a boy helped him to be a rider?
a) Yes, he felt he had to compensate for his speech difficulty.
b) No, he had a natural talent, but if his father hadn't helped and encouraged him, David might not have had the chance to develop it.
c) Yes, when David fell he developed special psychic powers.

Q: What do you think makes Sarah Bowen a top-class show-jumper?
a) She gets lots of practice as her dad is a show-jumper too.
b) She loves show-jumping and horses, so she tries hard.
c) Sarah has telepathic powers like her father.

TEST YOUR PET'S PSYCHIC POWERS: TEST 3

CAN YOUR PET SEE GHOSTS?

This test is designed to discover whether your pet can see ghosts or spirits. There is no absolute proof that such things exist, but who really knows? Perhaps this simple experiment with your pet may produce evidence that ghosts do walk the land.

Warning: DO NOT ATTEMPT THIS TEST ALONE!
For this test you will need a parent or guardian to observe and note the results. When searching for ghosts you must not go without an adult: it could be dangerous. Besides, if you or your pet see a ghost and you haven't got a grown-up with you, no one will believe you later when you tell them about it.

Haunted houses and mysterious mansions

Everywhere in the world there are reports of spooky castles or houses that have ghosts. Many believe that hauntings happen when the spirits of those who once lived there return to visit their previous homes. Your pet may be able to see or sense the presence of such ghosts. Now you can discover whether your pet is a psychic ghost hunter.

No, not the snake!

Cats and dogs especially are thought to have the psychic power to see spirits. It is not advisable to try the experiment with a bird or a small creature such as a mouse or lizard. If someone lives in the haunted house, they surely wouldn't want you setting them loose there.

1) Research

First you need to locate the nearest haunted house or mansion. Ask a librarian for books on local history and for the address of your area's local-history society—there probably is one.

Write to this society, basing your letter on the samples. If there is something like a famous mansion in your neighborhood, you will obviously already know that. So just ask whether it is thought to have any ghosts and, if so, what kind. Enclose a stamped, self-addressed envelope when you mail the letter.

While waiting for their reply, read up on local history to give you an idea of what to expect. If there turns out to be no suitable place to hunt ghosts in your area, maybe you can persuade your family to make a weekend outing to somewhere further away. Tell them it is educational.

13 Spook Street
Anytown
Zip code
USA
date

Director
Anytown Local History Society
Gallows Street
Ghost Town
Zip code
USA

Dear Sir or Madam,

I am interested in local history and especially in famous haunted houses. Can you please tell me where the nearest one is? Especially any haunted old mansions. I would also like to know whether your society has published any books that contain reference to local haunted houses.

I would appreciate any help that you can give me in locating a famous haunted place, because I am working on a project. I have enclosed a stamped, addressed envelope for your reply and look forward to hearing from you.

Sincerely,

(sign your name)

2) Arrange your ghost hunt

Having located a haunted house or mansion, you must now make an appointment to visit it with your pet **AND A PARENT OR GUARDIAN**. It is unlikely that you will be able simply to walk into a famous haunted house with a dog or cat.

Here is another sample letter to help you to arrange an appointment. Put in your own address, your pet's name and so on as appropriate. Again, don't forget to enclose a stamped, self-addressed envelope. Make it a fairly large one if you are asking them to send leaflets.

13 Spook Street
Anytown
Zip code
USA
date

The Caretaker
Castle Dracula
East West Street
Draculaland

Dear Sir or Madam,

I have read about your famous haunted house and am curious to discover whether ghosts exist. In a book published by Beyond Words Publishing I have read that pets may be able to see spirits. This interests me a great deal and I would like to bring my bulldog Rover to test this.

Will you please consider letting me visit your haunted house with my mom and Rover? He is a very well-behaved dog. I understand I may have to pay an entrance fee.

I have enclosed a stamped, addressed envelope for your reply and would be grateful also for any brochure or printed details you can send me. I look forward to hearing from you.

Sincerely,

(sign your name)

3) Final preparations

It is the day of your visit. Check that your parent or guardian hasn't forgotten that he or she promised to come with you to observe and make notes.

Next, prepare your pet. Make sure it takes no food for at least six hours before this test. Talk gently to it and promise it a treat afterwards. Make sure, too, that it has emptied its bowels. Ghostly goings-on might scare it a bit and you don't want an embarrassing accident on the carpet of the haunted home.

4) Into the haunted house

When you enter the house, you must thank the owner or caretaker for letting you in. Take a look around and show interest. Then lead your pet to the area where ghosts have been seen. Your adult observer must at all times watch your pet carefully and note its reactions, using the following form, which you should copy.

PSYCHIC PET GHOST-HUNT REPORT

Name of observer: Mr/Ms

_____

Date: day _____ month _____year _____

Location of haunted house:

_____

_____

_____

Name of pet _____

Breed _____

Name of owner _____

Address of owner

_____

_____

_____

_____

Observe and check boxes as you see fit.

Outside the entry to haunted house:

Pet seems quiet ☐

alert ☐

uneasy ☐

seeing something ☐

uh-oh! ☐

Inside haunted house:

Pet seems quiet ☐

alert ☐

uneasy ☐

seeing something ☐

uh-oh! ☐

At site of haunting:

Pet seems quiet ☐

alert ☐

uneasy ☐

seeing something ☐

uh-oh! ☐

Did pet do any of the following at any time during the ghost hunt?

Stare into vacant space as if observing something ☐

Jump up or snarl and growl at an invisible thing ☐

Cower away or seem very uneasy or even frightened ☐

Refuse to go near any area, especially one where ghost was said to have been seen ☐

Seem to be hearing a sound you couldn't hear ☐

Further observations

Did you notice any of the following?

Change in room temperature ☐

Sudden blast of cold air ☐

Feeling uneasy, as if you were entering the
twilight zone ☐

Weird or unaccountable sounds ☐

The feel of some invisible being watching you ☐

Feel something unseen touch you ☐

Appearance of white mist or something similar ☐

Full manifestation of ghost ☐

Additional observations

I noticed the following:

_____

_____

_____

_____

_____

_____

_____

_____

In my opinion the pet saw something I could not explain

Yes ☐

No ☐

I think that the above-named pet has psychic ghost-hunting powers

Yes ☐

No ☐

Signed:

_____

THE DOG THAT PLAYED WITH GHOSTS

Wendy and Louise own a beautiful Victorian house. From their collie dog Bob they found out that the house was haunted by the spirits of two children.

Bob is spooked

It all started late in January 1996. Wendy was fast asleep and Bob was snoozing on the rug at the foot of her bed. Suddenly he leaped up, ran out of the room and stood at the top of the stairs barking. Wendy woke up, wondering what on earth was the matter, and got out of bed to see what was going on.

Bob was at the top of the stairs, his fur raised. He barked and barked. He was gazing alternately down towards the hallway below and up at Wendy as if to say, "Look at that!"   She could see nothing, but around the stairway there was a distinct chill in the air, as if someone had opened the fridge door. Wendy could not understand what Bob was barking at, but he would not stop.

Then Bob ran downstairs, and she followed him. The long room there used to be two but the dividing wall had been removed by previous owners. From side to side he chased, looking into what had been the corners of the front room before the house was altered. His eyes were wide with surprise and he seemed to be looking at something only he could see.

Wendy thought that perhaps Bob could sense someone outside in the yard. Although fearing that it might be a burglar, she opened the back door. Outside, all was quiet. The moonbeams glistened silver on the still, cold yard. Whatever the reason for the dog's alarm, it was not to be found out there. In the end, Wendy gave up and went back to bed.

An invisible guitar player

The next morning at the breakfast table, over tea, toast and marmalade, Wendy and Louise discussed the night's disturbance. Unable to think of a better explanation, they decided Bob must have had a bad dream. Having agreed on that, they thought no more about it and set off to work.

That night, as the old cottage lay in darkness and all within slept peacefully, it happened again. At three in the morning Bob woke the house with his barking, and once more he stood at the top of the stairs looking first up and then down. The fur on his back was almost standing on end. Wendy again searched the house and the yard, finding nothing.

The next morning both ladies were very tired, having been kept awake by Bob's barking and by wondering what was really causing it.

The next night, just as Wendy and Louise were going to bed, they heard the sound of Louise's acoustic guitar being strummed. Someone or something was tinkling the strings, and the sound came from the rooms downstairs. Bob jumped up, raced down the stairs and dashed into the living room. Wendy and Louise ran after him, certain that this time they would catch the culprit.

In the lounge Bob was leaping from side to side as if he were playing with someone, and still barking. The room was icy cold, although the heating had been on and all the rest of the cottage was warm. Wendy looked at Louise, grabbed Bob by the collar and together they ran out of the room.

That night neither Wendy nor Louise slept a wink. Both were now convinced that their home was haunted.

The medium meets the ghosts

Wendy and Louise have a friend who is a psychic spiritualist medium. If their house was haunted, this woman, Lesley Shepherd, would know what to do, they thought. So Louise called her on the phone.

Having listened to Louise tell her story, Lesley Shepherd agreed to visit the house and use her psychic powers to search for any spirit presence. She promised Louise that she would ask her friends in the spirit world to look at their home and, if there were any ghosts visiting, to make sure they were there when she arrived.

Early next Sunday afternoon, Lesley came to the house. Bob had been taken to stay with friends until Wendy and Louise solved the problem. They just could not stand any more nights of disturbed sleep. As soon as Lesley entered the house, she sensed the presence of two spirit children.

As she walked into the large downstairs room, she saw them. A barefooted boy, who said he was called Tom, held the hand of a little spirit girl who said her name was Jenny. They looked about nine and seven years old and were dressed in rags and tatters. They had, they said, lived in the cottage a long time ago. Their family had been very poor and there was not enough to eat, so they had died of hunger.

Tom told Lesley (who could hear through her gift of clairaudience) that they had come back to their old home to play with the nice dog. They said they hid in the corners of the room and teased the collie. Jenny thought it was a lot of fun. They had never had any pets when they were alive.

Now Lesley had a word with them. She explained—through her thoughts—that they were upsetting the new owners of the cottage and frightening the dog. When she had finished, both Tom and Jenny agreed not to do it again. They had only been playing and really did not mean any harm.

From that afternoon on, the house has rested in peace. No more are the nights disturbed by the barks of Bob the collie, who was once the playmate of two ghost children. Lesley Shepherd says they have returned to their home in the land that awaits us all beyond this material world.

PSYCHIC ASSESSMENT

Q: Why do you think Bob the dog was barking and looking down the stairs?
a) He had a bad dream.
b) He sensed the presence of something strange.
c) He could see the spirit children.

Q: Why did Wendy and Louise think their cottage was haunted?
a) They had heard about hauntings from their friend Lesley.
b) Because Louise heard her guitar being played.
c) Both Wendy and Louise felt a supernatural coldness whenever Bob was barking at an unseen presence.

Q: How could Lesley Shepherd see Tom and Jenny, the spirit children?
a) Lesley did not see anything, she made it all up.
b) Lesley imagined she saw Tom and Jenny.
c) Lesley is a psychic spiritualist medium who has a special gift that enables her to tune into the spirit world.

Q: If there is a heavenly afterworld, why would the children come back for the pleasure of teasing a dog?
a) Some people will make up very crazy explanations for a dog barking.
b) Heaven is rather a dull place.
c) They were naughty children but they are at peace now.

SHANDY THE PSYCHIC LABRADOR

Lesley Ann Wadsworth ran boarding kennels for many years with her family. She told me this eerie story about one of her regular customers.

"Over a number of years the Jones family had been boarding Shandy, their pet Labrador, in our kennels while they went away on vacation. The dog was a huge, friendly thing, all golden brown and cuddly. We knew Shandy really well and he seemed to enjoy his stay at our kennels.

"Shandy always slept well at night. He would run around all day playing and in addition he was always taken on a long walk, so by evening he was tired out and rested well. Then, on the night before he was due to be picked up, in the early hours Shandy started to howl.

"I had never heard the dog make such a terrible racket before. He howled and cried, waking all the other pets up. Like us, they must have wondered what on earth was wrong. I went to see him in his kennel but Shandy would not be comforted. All night he howled and none of us got back to sleep.

"The next morning I received a telephone call from a close relative of the Jones family. They said that the dog could not be picked up that day because Mr. and Mrs. Jones had been killed in a car crash on their way back from their vacation. The accident had happened at 3 a.m.—exactly the time Shandy had started to howl!"

PSYCHIC ASSESSMENT

Q: Why do you think Shandy was howling in the kennels?

a) Stomach ache.

b) Shandy was missing his family and thought they had abandoned him.

c) Shandy telepathically sensed that his owners had been killed and cried out in sadness.

MYTHS AND LEGENDS OF SUPERNATURAL CATS

Cats have always been thought of as mystical creatures with psychic powers. Perhaps it is the strange look they have in their eyes, almost as if they know something we don't.

Mythology of cats

● The ancient Egyptians had a cat goddess called Bast. There were many temples and even a whole city, Bubastis, dedicated to her worship. In May a festival was held in her honor.

All cats in the early Egyptian culture were considered to be sacred creatures that could speak to the spirits. To kill a cat meant certain execution.

● One of the old Norse gods worshipped in Scandinavia over a thousand years ago was a goddess called Freya, ruler of fertility and death. Beautiful and generous, she was closely associated with cats and her chariot was drawn by them.

● Certain Australian Aborigines have the wild cat as a totem animal that they believe represents the spirit of their tribe.

● The Chinese traditionally believe the cat to be a creature of the night, an animal of darkness. In terms of Yin and Yang, the two poles of the life force, cats came under the heading of Yin, the dark and passive aspect.

Witches' cats

In the Middle Ages, many people believed in witchcraft. Those accused were usually women, and their pet cats were said to be their familiar spirits. Especially black cats were believed to be the host to demons or devils that controlled the witch.

Under torture, some accused witches even claimed to be able to change themselves into cats and walk the night.

In 1718, William Montgomery of Scotland, reported being attacked by witches who had changed themselves into cats. One moonless night, his story went, he woke to hear the cries of a pack of cats outside his home. When he went to investigate, a number of these tried to scratch him. Picking up an axe which happened to be lying nearby, he defended himself, killing two of the cats and injuring others.

The next day two old ladies from his village were found dead in their beds, and another had a wound in her leg that she refused to explain. William Montgomery asserted that these were witches who had turned themselves into cats to attack him.

Cat superstitions

Black cats are, in many parts of the world, thought to be lucky. However in the USA and in some other European countries, black cats are considered bad omens.

In England they say that it is lucky to have a black cat cross your path. Well, it is not so simple. There is a belief that this is lucky only if the cat crosses from right to left. If it crosses from left to right, or halts and turns back halfway, then bad luck is believed to follow.

In America, a white cat is thought to be lucky, but in Great Britain such creatures are considered bad news.

In many parts of the world, the behavior of cats is used to foretell the weather. When cats chase around in a hurry, dashing here and there, bad weather is supposed to be on the way. And when a cat is seen washing its ears, a storm is due. Some say that when a cat eats grass, rain is imminent.

In China, it was believed that when the household cat rubs its face with its paw, visitors are coming.

One strange belief about cats is that they can sense death approaching. Some believe that cats will not stay in a house that has death within. If there is illness in a house and the cat leaves and will not return, the sick person will surely die, they say.

Sailors at sea believe that ship's cats are very lucky, though they never speak their names. If a ship's cat falls overboard, it is believed that a violent storm is certain.

In the theater, actors dread seeing a cat run across the stage. It is supposed to bring great misfortune to the performance.

Miners in the coal fields will not pronounce the word "cat" while working underground.

In the tin mines, miners believe that if a cat is found down a pit, then tragedy must follow.

One old tradition is that if the family cat sneezes on a bride on her wedding day, she is certain to have a happy married life.

But cat sneezes are not always lucky. If a cat sneezes three times, then, according to tradition, all the members of the household will soon catch colds.

Cat cures

Often cats have been thought to have psychic healing powers.

An ancient cure for warts was three drops of blood taken from a cat and rubbed into the wart's surface.

Another cure for warts was rubbing them with a tortoiseshell cat's tail, though this was supposed to work only in the month of May.

Stroking with a black cat's tail, on the other hand, was recommended for a sore eye.

Needless to say, such cures do not work at all.

Some people held that washing a sick person and then throwing the bath water over a cat transferred the illness to the cat. The poor creature must then be chased out of the house, if it hadn't already run off in a huff.

Cat history

In the tenth century, Wales was ruled by King Hywel. Recognizing the worth of cats as catchers and killers of mice, he made a law that no one may hurt or kill a cat on the pain of severe punishment. He was known as Hywel the Good— especially among cat lovers.

The pantomime story of Dick Whittington's cat is based on fact. Whittington, three times Lord Mayor of London, did by all accounts own a black cat. And it is evident that it brought him great good luck.

The Polish-born Queen Marie of France, wife of Louis XV, made an order that cats were to have the freedom of the capital city of Paris. All French people were warned never to injure a cat, or else!

THE CURSE OF TOOTY

In the county of Essex in England there lives a black tom cat called Tooty. His owners Andy and Penny Boot told me of their pet's amazing psychic powers.

The story starts in 1980 when Tooty first came to live with Andy and his wife Penny. They had a home and were both struggling to earn a living as writers, always a difficult task.

Stroke a cat, make a wish

In November that year, the atmosphere in the Boots' home was desperate. There were more bills than money and Andy wondered how he would find the cash to buy food. Penny was fed up with being poor and Andy was close to despair.

Over a late-night cup of tea, Andy picked up Tooty, petted him and told him his troubles. Stroking the cat's deep-black fur, he looked into Tooty's mysterious green eyes and whispered, "Help us, Tooty! We're broke."

As he gently rubbed the little cat's back, Tooty suddenly bristled. His eyes were shining like two lumps of bright-green jade. Andy wondered what the little creature was thinking.

Two days later a check for many hundreds of dollars arrived in the mail. It was payment for the Japanese rights to a book Andy had written years before and almost forgotten about.

Tooty the cat-finder

One day the Boots' other cat, a tabby tom called Spangle, went for a walk and failed to return. After thirty-six hours he was still missing and they were worried. Then Penny had an idea. She picked up Tooty and said to him, "Go find Spangle."

For a second Tooty stiffened in her arms and his eyes flashed brilliant green. He jumped down from Penny's knee and ran out of the door.

It was almost midnight when Penny heard the bedroom door squeak open. There in the doorway stood Tooty. He strolled in and curled up at the bottom of the bed, his usual place.

Two minutes later, in walked Spangle. Tooty had been out, found him and brought him back.

Nellie the bully

Tooty also has a darker side to his psychic powers. If anyone hurts him or his friends, Tooty takes action. How he does this is beyond explanation; certainly Penny and Andy don't know. But they have seen the curse of Tooty working. It is bad news for those who cross his path, be they animal or human.

The first time they witnessed this was in 1990 when Nellie joined the Boot family. She was a huge black and white female cat, twice the size of Tooty. Nellie was a big bully of a cat. She would walk up to wherever Tooty was sitting and push him out of the way. If he didn't move, Nellie used to lie down on top of him, crushing the poor little creature.

One morning Andy saw Nellie on top of Tooty and went to pull her off. The black tom cat was half dead and had difficulty breathing. As Andy stroked him, he gasped for breath. Then he grew tense, all his fur stiffened and he looked straight at Nellie with green fire in his eyes.

As soon as Nellie saw the look on Tooty's face, she ran out of the house with her tail in the air. From that day to this no one has seen Nellie: she just disappeared.

Jasper the flirt

Next, the Boot family decided to buy a dog. They got a big friendly hound they called Jasper. Now Jasper took quite a liking to Tooty—too much so. He would creep up behind the black tom cat and his intentions were not those of a gentleman. Tooty objected, and quite right too.

For a few weeks the cat put up with Jasper's unwanted attention. But one day he suddenly turned. Jasper had just walked towards the cat when Tooty shot forwards, across the room. Again his dark eyes sparkled with emerald venom. The dog whimpered as though it had been hit, then crawled quietly into a corner and lay perfectly still.

That afternoon when Andy took Jasper out for his daily walk, the dog ran away. No sooner had Andy let him off the leash than the dog bolted into the distance. And that was the last they ever saw of him.

Back at home, Tooty was quietly contented. He snuggled up to Penny and seemed to be smiling, as if the cat knew that Jasper had gone for ever.

Tooty's revenge

It was when the Boot family decided to move to a new home that the very weirdest thing happened.

Knowing how much Tooty loved their garden at their old

house, Andy chose a nice house that had a big garden. They even took Tooty to have a look and he seemed to like it. Then things started to go wrong. The inspector who was called in to make a report on the property made some major mistakes.

When inspectors reports are wrong, they can cause a lot of trouble. Just ask Andy and Penny. They lost their ideal home and had to move to a tiny little place with no garden. Tooty didn't like it at all.

On the night they moved in, Andy could have cried. His pet had nowhere to play and the house was so small. He picked Tooty up and told him what had happened. The black cat's eyes glowed green as Andy spoke of the inspector whose fault this was.

A few days later, Andy had cause to telephone the office of the inspector who had messed the move up. The inspector's receptionist told him that the man who had been dealing with their property had suddenly been taken seriously ill. He was not expected to work again.

Andy put the phone down and went to tell his wife. Before he could do so, he saw Tooty the cat, sitting on a chair and staring at the telephone. His eyes were sparkling with a strange green light, as if he knew.

Tooty is seventeen years old now and still lives with Andy and Penny. Andy told me that they treat him with great respect—no wonder!

PSYCHIC ASSESSMENT

Q: When Penny asked Tooty to go find Spangle, how did he do it?

a) Tooty just accidentally met Spangle in the street outside.

b) Tooty knew where Spangle usually went.

c) Tooty used his psychic powers to tune in and find Spangle.

Q: Do you think Tooty really put a curse on the inspector?

a) No, though Andy and Penny must have cursed him a great deal.

b) Maybe all the ill feeling he had caused, from both humans and animals, rebounded on him.

c) Yes. Some cats have strong psychic powers and can use these for good or evil.

GYPSY THE SINGING CAT

There is a theory that pets can help make sick people better. Some say they have special psychic powers that are transmitted to their poorly owners, healing them. Others believe that just by loving a pet, human beings become strong, as though the force of love makes them better.

A cat for Carol

Carol Taylor was a very sick lady. Doctors had told her she might never be able to walk again.

One bright summer afternoon in July 1985, two boys called Colin and Tom, who lived next door to Carol, found a lost cat in the woods near her house. The tiny tabby was very thin and looked as if it needed some milk. Colin, who was the eldest, suggested they take it Carol. They knew she was a kind person who loved pets.

Carol was delighted and gave the cat a bowl of her Sunday

special cream. It lapped it up, then curled itself into a contented ball and was soon asleep at her feet.

Carol called her new pet Gypsy, because he had been a wandering cat.

Gypsy melodies

Gypsy no longer wandered; he quickly became Carol's best friend. She would feed him fish and milk during the week and each Sunday he had a cream treat. In next to no time, Gypsy had become a strong, fit cat with a coat that shone with health and vitality. Carol loved her cat and she knew that Gypsy loved her.

Each night he would lie next to her on the bed and make a strange singing sound deep inside his throat. This friendly noise calmed Carol, who would drift into peaceful sleep comforted by the song of her cat.

Then the strangest thing happened: Carol began to get well. Her illness, which had prevented her from walking properly, gradually disappeared. She was sleeping better now, and the pain and weakness she had felt in her arms and legs was gone. She believed it had been lifted from her by the love she received from Gypsy the singing cat.

Phone for you, kitty!

Some two years after Gypsy had come into her life, Carol was able to go back to work as an accountant. The doctors who had said she could not be cured were amazed. But Carol missed her friend Gypsy while she was away in the office. They had spent so much time together that Carol thought he might now be lonely. Then she had an idea.

To enable her to speak to Gypsy from work, she bought a telephone answering machine. She turned the volume up and placed it near Gypsy's favorite chair. That way, when she telephoned from the office, Gypsy could hear her voice as she spoke to him.

Carol knew that Gypsy was listening to the calls she made. At night he would climb up on the table where the answering machine was and rub his little head against it. As he did so, Gypsy would sing his happy song and look with his deep green eyes at Carol. She knew there was love in that gentle stare, and in her heart she could feel that Gypsy was saying thank you for thinking about him.

The years passed and Carol's friendship with Gypsy the cat grew and grew. Each night he would curl around her feet and purr contentedly as she sat watching television or reading a book. At bedtime Gypsy still sang his strange, comforting song, soft, sweet murmurings that seemed to ease all the tension out of Carol's body and let her drift away into a refreshing, dreamless sleep.

A sad loss

Then, in 1992, Gypsy was taken ill. Carol rushed him to the vet at once, and he promised he would try to save her cat. Gypsy's once shining green eyes dimmed as Carol stroked him one last time and placed his weary body into the veterinary surgeon's hands.

At home, once more alone, Carol could not sleep. Her mind went back to that day seven years ago when the two boys from next door had brought her the singing cat. She had been a very

sick and lonely lady then, and Gypsy had saved her. The love she had received from him had given her the strength to survive. Now all she could do was wait, wait and pray that God would look after her friend, just as he had looked after her.

Near dawn, Carol had a vision of her cat. She saw herself standing with Gypsy, holding him in her arms and listening to his soft voice tenderly purring his song of joy. Instantly she awoke. Glancing across the room, she saw that the clock said 4:02 a.m.

Something deep inside told her that Gypsy had died, and she cried. No more would she hear his happy murmurings or stroke his golden-brown fur. At nine that morning she telephoned the vet's office, and her suspicion was confirmed. Gypsy had died, they said, at two minutes past four, the exact time she had the vision of holding him.

A recorded message from the other side

In the months following the loss of Gypsy, Carol struggled to come to terms with her life alone, but it was hard. She went to a small clinic that helped people manage their personal problems. Brenda, the woman who ran the clinic, offered to make Carol a special cassette tape of music and kind words to help her sleep at night.

Some days later Brenda phoned Carol to say the audio cassette was ready if she would like to pick it up. Some weird sounds had appeared on the tape, Brenda said, in addition to the music she recorded. She did not know what the sounds were but she had left them on for Carol to hear.

That night when Carol got back from the clinic, she put the tape into her cassette player and switched it on. As she lay back on the bed, listening to the gentle music, she heard a strange but familiar sound. It was Gypsy's voice singing his song of love and contentment.

At first Carol could not believe it. Stopping the tape, she rewound it and listened again. It was definitely the contented murmurings of Gypsy the singing cat that she heard on the tape.

It was as if he had returned to help her once again, just when she needed him, offering her comfort with his sweet, soft song.

The sound of Gypsy's voice made Carol realize that the love they had shared would never die and that life must go on. The singing cat had taught her many, many things in its short time on earth: how to love and be loved, how to give and receive joy. Her friend had made Carol understand that there is peace and tranquility to be found for all who care to look past the tears of today's troubles. Even from beyond this world, Gypsy had reached her. Carol would never more be sad and lonely. She knew that love and life are eternal and that in time to come she would listen once more to the beautiful voice of her beloved singing cat.

PSYCHIC ASSESSMENT

Q: How did Carol get better after Gypsy had come to live with her?

a) Her illness had run its course.

b) The cat gave her something to live for.

c) The cat used its psychic healing powers.

Q: Why do you think Gypsy the cat sang to Carol?

a) Because he was a happy and contented cat.

b) Because he knew she enjoyed hearing him sing.

c) To express his love for her.

Q: When Gypsy died and Carol had a vision in which she held him in her arms, what do you think was really happening?

a) Carol was having a vivid dream.

b) Gypsy was telepathically telling Carol he was alright even though he was dead.

c) Carol and Gypsy actually met in their spirit bodies.

Q: How did Carol hear the sound of Gypsy's singing on the cassette?

a) It was just a distortion that sounded like a cat purring.

b) It was an echo in Carol's mind.

c) From the spirit world Gypsy sang on to the tape.

TEST YOUR PET'S PSYCHIC POWERS: TEST 4

IS YOUR PET CLAIRVOYANT?

These tests are designed to discover if your pet has psychic sight. It involves you, the pet owner, in a series of experiments that must be carefully recorded. Each test should be repeated at least three times over three days, with the results logged on the record sheet provided.

Test 1: The biscuit in the envelope

For this test you will need the following:

4	ordinary envelopes
1	biscuit or chew (your pet's favourite)
3	pieces of cardboard cut to same size as the biscuit or chew
	plastic wrap or tin foil
	tape

Step 1: Mark the envelopes "A", "B", "C", "D".

Step 2: Wrap the biscuit or chew in plastic wrap or foil to prevent your pet detecting it by smell.

Step 3: Place the biscuit or chew in the envelope marked "A". Seal the envelope.

Step 4: Place cardboard cutouts in the other three envelopes and seal them.

Step 5: Place the envelopes on the floor with a few feet between each.

Step 6: Call your pet forward and say, "Find the chew/biscuit!"

Step 7: Make a note on the test log of which envelope your pet selects.

Repeat steps 1 to 7 two more times.

Test 2: The dinner in the box

For this test you will need the following:

> 4 cardboard boxes, roughly the same size
>
> a bowl of your pet's favorite food
>
> plastic wrap or a clean plastic bag
>
> tape

Step 1: Mark the boxes "A", "B", "C", "D".

Step 2: Wrap bowl of food in plastic wrap or place in clean plastic bag, then seal with tape.

Step 3: Place the bowl of food in the box marked "A".

Step 4: Seal all the boxes as tightly as you can with tape.

Step 5: Place the boxes on the floor with a few feet between each.

Step 6: Call your pet forward and say, "Find dinner" or whatever.

Step 7: Make a note on the test log of which box your pet selects.

Repeat steps 1 to 7 two more times, moving the boxes each time.

TEST LOG

Name of pet _____

Breed _____

Name of owner _____

Dates of test 1:   Dates of test 2:

day __ month ____year ____   day __ month ____year ____

day __ month ____year ____   day __ month ____year ____

day __ month ____year ____   day __ month ____year ____

Place a check next to the letter matching the envelope or box your pet selected.

Test 1: The biscuit   **Test 2: The dinner**

DAY ONE:

A ☐ B ☐ C ☐ D ☐   A ☐ B ☐ C ☐ D ☐

A ☐ B ☐ C ☐ D ☐   A ☐ B ☐ C ☐ D ☐

A ☐ B ☐ C ☐ D ☐   A ☐ B ☐ C ☐ D ☐

DAY TWO

A ☐ B ☐ C ☐ D ☐   A ☐ B ☐ C ☐ D ☐

A ☐ B ☐ C ☐ D ☐   A ☐ B ☐ C ☐ D ☐

A ☐ B ☐ C ☐ D ☐   A ☐ B ☐ C ☐ D ☐

DAY THREE

A ☐ B ☐ C ☐ D ☐   A ☐ B ☐ C ☐ D ☐

A ☐ B ☐ C ☐ D ☐   A ☐ B ☐ C ☐ D ☐

A ☐ B ☐ C ☐ D ☐   A ☐ B ☐ C ☐ D ☐

RESULTS: Total all "A" selections and refer to table below.

14–18	"A" selections: Your pet has highly developed psychic sight, or knows the alphabet.
10–13	"A" selections: Your pet has good psychic sight.
6–9	"A" selections: Your pet has some psychic sight.
0–5	"A" selections: Your pet is about as psychic as a banana.

FINN McCOULL AND RORY, THE TELEPORTING PETS

Sandy Robertson is a psychic researcher. She loves pets and believes that they have many supernatural powers. Sandy lives with her husband Adrian, a ginger tom cat called Finn McCoull, and a big Border collie called Rory.

A good judge of character

Sandy and Adrian were invited to a friend's home. They took along Rory, who enjoys riding in the car. At the house, Rory sat quietly until suddenly there came a knock at the door. At once he started to bark and all the fur on his back stood up.

When the lady of the house opened the door, a woman came in and introduced herself to Sandy. Rory was going bonkers, barking, snarling and woofing like mad. Adrian tried to calm the dog but Rory would not stop. He was extremely distressed by the woman. It was as if he could sense something evil.

In less than a week, the woman that Sandy had met began to cause terrible trouble for her and Adrian. At night she would telephone, pestering Sandy. Strangely, as soon as the phone rang, Rory would start barking and his fur would raise. It was almost as though he knew who was at the other end of the line.

Sandy is sure that Rory can sense wickedness in a person. If only she had paid attention when her dog started barking at that woman, she says, a great deal of trouble could have been avoided.

Beam me up, kitty!

According to Sandy Robertson, both Rory and Finn McCoull have the ability to transport themselves by supernatural means. She believes that both her cat and her dog have apported from place to place: disappearing from one location and appearing in another.

For example, one evening late in October 1995, Sandy was feeling very tired and wanted to go to bed early. She asked Adrian to lock up and put the pets to bed. He assures me that this is exactly what he did. This is his account of Finn McCoull's apport.

"Rory the dog always sleeps in the living room. I left him a bowl of water and closed the door at about 10 p.m. Then I carried Finn McCoull, who had been sleeping on my knee, into the kitchen, placed him in his box, checked he had water, stroked his head, closed the door and went to bed.

"It was about three in the morning when I awoke. Something was swinging the light switch, which is a long length of string fitted to a socket in the ceiling. I stared into the darkness, waking Sandy as I did. I felt there might be a burglar in the room. Then I reached out and grabbed the still swinging string, pulled it and the light came on. There on the bedside table was Finn McCoull."

There was no natural way the ginger tom cat could have got into the room. Adrian had closed the bedroom door before going to sleep, the window was also closed, and anyway he had shut Finn McCoull into the kitchen before he went to bed.

Rory joins the seance

Sandy once went to investigate a haunted house. In her role as a psychic researcher, she sat in on a seance in which a group of mediums tried to call forth the spirit haunting the house. They sat there in a circle concentrating their psychic powers.

"We were expecting to receive a message from the spirit world, telling us who was haunting this house. Suddenly I heard one medium shout, 'Look, a dog!' When I turned I could clearly see Rory standing in the far corner of the room, wagging his tail. He looked happy and started to walk towards me, but halfway across the room he just vanished into thin air. We all saw this. I'm sure he teleported himself from home."

Adrian believes that Rory is linked on a psychic level to Sandy. Perhaps Sandy's work as a psychic researcher has tuned her in to the pets' vibrations and they are using this attunement to apport.

PSYCHIC ASSESSMENT

Q: Why did Rory start barking at the woman?
a)   Dogs always bark at strangers.
b)   Rory wanted attention.
c)   Rory could sense that this woman was evil.

Q: How did Finn McCoull get into the closed
     bedroom?
a)   The cat followed Adrian upstairs.
b)   Adrian didn't shut the doors properly.
c)   Finn McCoull apported himself using his psychic powers.

Q: What really happened at the haunted house?
a)   A dog outside the house was reflected in a mirror.
b)   Sandy and the mediums imagined seeing a dog.
c)   Rory used Sandy's psychic vibrations to apport.

THE EXORCIST

In a seaside town, there lives a man whose duty it is to deal with hauntings on behalf of the Church. The Reverend Tom Willis is a quietly spoken, silver-haired gentleman in his mid-sixties, and he has been, for over thirty years, an official exorcist.

He believes that animals are especially psychic and has no doubt that pets have some kind of extra sense that allows them to see spirits. He has met many people who say that sometimes their pets stare into mid-air as if they can see something that is not there. Or is it? Although he says he has never seen a ghost himself, he is sure that there are such things. He has conducted the ceremony of exorcism many hundreds of times, commanding ghosts, spirits, poltergeists and other unearthly presences to return to their appointed place. This is one of his stories.

Sparky the terrier
In the early 1990s a couple, Mary and Jack, were living with their cross-breed terrier Sparky. One day in October, Sparky had been playing in the living room with Mary. She was throwing his

favorite ball and the dog chased it round the room. Suddenly they heard footsteps thudding along the upstairs landing. Sparky raced out of the room and ran upstairs. Mary followed, but rather uneasily. As far as she knew, there was no one in the house but her and the dog.

As she walked towards the door leading into the corridor, she heard Sparky give out an almighty yelp. Mary steeled herself to look for an intruder. She searched the whole house, but could find no one, though she eventually discovered Sparky cowering under the bed.

The greaser's ghost

It was some days later, during which time Sparky had refused to go upstairs, that Mary saw the ghost. Early one morning as she went to get the milk from the front doorstep, she heard once again the mysterious footsteps. Turning round, she could clearly see a figure standing at the top of the stairs.

He was dressed in the style of the 1950s: straight pants with a black leather jacket. His hair was slicked back. Boys who dressed this way were called "greasers", because they greased their hair back. It was associated with the early days of rock and roll.

Over the following weeks, Mary saw the spirit time and again. She grew so frightened that she would not go upstairs alone. Jack, her husband, really thought she was putting all this ghost stuff on, until he himself encountered the spirit late one night after he had been watching TV. As he walked along the hall leading to the stairs, he saw a weird light flickering at the top. Inside the glow stood the spectre of the greaser. That night he could hardly sleep.

Jack asked the neighbors whether they had any idea who the ghost might be. He was told that in the 1950s there had been a car accident outside the house. In the crash a young man, dressed just as Mary described, had died. This was too much for Jack, and he sent for the exorcist.

Sparky flips out

As the Reverend Tom Willis walked along the path leading to the family home, he saw shards of broken glass scattered everywhere. Reaching the door, he could see where these came from: the bottom glass panel had been shattered. Inside he was told, by a very frightened Mary, just what had happened.

She had been upstairs making the beds with Jack. Hearing the dog bark downstairs, she went to the landing to see what was wrong. As soon as he saw her, Sparky headed up the stairs. Suddenly the ghost was there. Sparky turned around, almost flew down the steps, leaped forward and crashed straight through the bottom glass panel of the door and disappeared down the street. Mary, who clearly saw the spirit of the greaser, almost fainted. Just then, the exorcist approached.

Exorcism

Gathering the family together in the main room, the Reverend Willis called upon the ghost to leave the house. As they stood, trembling and holding hands, the exorcist commanded the spirit to go back to his appointed place.

There was a deep coldness in the air as the exorcist blessed the house. As he prayed aloud, Mary saw the outline of the ghostly greaser, but it quickly began to fade. Gradually it dimmed and finally vanished into the fast-falling twilight of that cold night, never to be seen again.

Sparky the terrier later returned and was none the worse for his experience.

PSYCHIC ASSESSMENT

Q: What do you think was the source of the footsteps?
a) Someone walking about next door.
b) An intruder.
c) The ghost.

Q: When Mary first saw the greaser, why did she assume it was a ghost and not a living person?
a) Because she had read lots of ghost stories.
b) Because no one dresses like that any more.
c) Because the house was locked and no one could have got in.

Q: Why did Sparky dive through the glass door panel?
a) He didn't. Mary and Jack broke the panel to make the exorcist believe them.
b) Something frightened the dog, but we don't know what it was.
c) He ran from the ghost.

Q: The Reverend Willis thinks pets are very psychic. What do you think?
a) Animals are sensitive to atmosphere, but there is nothing supernatural about it.
b) My pet often seems to see things I can't.
c) Animals are in touch with the spirit world.

LUCIFER
THE BOSS CAT

Elizabeth St. George is very fond of cats—she once had twelve of
them. They were, she says, under the control of a big black tom
cat called Lucifer. He was so intelligent that he knew how to
switch on the electric blanket in Elizabeth's bedroom. He could
then snuggle down into the covers and sleep. Even so, some of
his talents surprised her.

Kitty brigade

Lucifer had a great dislike of car travel. Since he was such a
beautiful cat, Elizabeth often entered him into cat shows. Less
often did she arrive at these with Lucifer. He somehow knew that
car travel was planned and disappeared through the cat-door on
the front door before she could catch him.

To keep him inside, Elizabeth decided to block off the cat-flap
the evening before one particular cat show. She placed a huge
five-gallon barrel of disinfectant in front of the cat-door, totally
blocking it.

The next morning, the barrel barricade had been pushed aside and Lucifer was gone.

Certainly Lucifer on his own could not have shifted the barricade. The drum must have weighed 20 pounds or more. The only way that barricade could have been moved was by the cats acting together as a team.

Elizabeth knew that Lucifer was in charge; she had seen him leading the others on a fridge raid. Some fridge doors can be opened by cats, if they are not too tight. Food kept going missing and her cats were looking plump, especially Lucifer. So Elizabeth decided to take precautions when she bought some steak for her Sunday lunch. On Saturday night she shut it into her oven, which had a very heavy door.

The next morning when Elizabeth opened the oven door, she was absolutely startled to find the plate that had held the steak empty. It would certainly have taken a gang of cats to open that heavy door, and the steak was far more than even a big tom like Lucifer could have eaten. The cats must have worked together as a team in both opening the oven and eating the contents. But imagine the cats being crafty enough to shut the door again!

It is generally believed that cats do not hunt in packs. However, Elizabeth believes that with Lucifer, the boss cat, in charge, her other pets obeyed his telepathic instructions. He seemed able to control them by the psychic power of his mind.

Very early one spring morning, just as dawn was breaking, Elizabeth's son was returning home. As he walked down the long pathway leading to the front door, he saw twelve cats in a pack hunting by the side of the trees. At the front was Lucifer. His eyes were blazing like green fire as he led his troop of cats in a search for wild, fresh food.

The girl who could not read

In a house across the street from Lucifer's home, there lived a girl called Anne who was having trouble with her lessons at school. At eight, she could not read or write, no matter how hard she tried. The teachers had told her parents that she was educationally below normal and would probably never be able to read or write. They sent Anne to a special school, away from all her friends.

Anne had cried and cried when her mother explained what had to happen to her. She didn't want to leave the school where all her pals from down her street went. She couldn't understand why they wanted to send her away. It seemed a punishment, and she knew she had done her best.

Then one afternoon as she walked sadly home from her special school, Lucifer the cat fell into step beside Anne. He followed her all the way home and into her house. As she ate her meal, Lucifer sat and watched. Anne liked the cat and fed him a few tidbits from her plate. Afterwards, when she went upstairs to start the heartbreakingly impossible homework, he followed.

That evening Lucifer watched as little Anne struggled with the funny symbols that she knew were words, though she could not read them. Then a strange thing happened: this night she could see a word and it seemed to make sense. It was just a simple word next to a picture. "Apple," she said out loud to Lucifer, and the cat seemed to smile. "Apple," she said again, with growing conviction. "Apple." Hearing this, Sally, Anne's mother, ran upstairs. She could hardly believe it—Anne was reading! For the first time in her life she had read a word.

From that day on Lucifer would meet Anne on her way home from her special school and, after a few morsels from her meal, he would follow her upstairs and sit by her side as she did her homework.

Days turned to weeks, weeks to months, and Anne gradually learned to read and write. Each night she would sit with the cat at her side and read her lessons aloud. Lucifer listened and the little girl got more and more confident. The teachers were amazed at her achievement. She could no longer be thought of as a below normal child—she was just Anne. It was all she had ever wanted, to be normal like everyone else.

For almost ten years Anne shared the love and friendship of Lucifer. Elizabeth St. George told me that both Anne and her mother Sally are quite certain that it was the cat that helped save Anne from failure. Somehow the tom cat had given her just what she needed: an uncomplaining, uncritical ear. He had listened patiently night after night as the little girl had struggled with her words.

Anne will never forget him. Today she has just passed her driving test and is well on her way in the world. But without Lucifer, Anne is sure this could never have happened.

A cat fit for a goddess

Lucifer's long life—he lived to be twenty-three—came slowly to an end. He had been a noble creature and Elizabeth loved him to the last. As she laid his weary body to rest in the shade of her garden, she remembered his goodness. Lowering him into his tiny grave, beneath a statue of Bast, the cat goddess, just as she had always promised him, Elizabeth said a little prayer for his soul.

As she whispered the last words, the final rays of the evening sun filtered through the trees, bathing the entire garden in a golden glow. She looked up and saw the most wondrous sight: a proud black cat glistening in the fast-fading sunbeams. The cat was standing on its hind legs, just like a human. She swears it was the spirit of Lucifer; she knows because she heard the ghost speak, thanking her for keeping the promise she had made, to bury his body in the shadow of Bast, the Egyptian cat goddess.

PSYCHIC ASSESSMENT

Q: How did Lucifer get out of the blocked cat-door?

a) He was running around with the other cats and they accidentally barged into the barrel and knocked it over.

b) He pushed at it half the night and moved it inch by inch.

c) He got the other cats to help him.

Q: How do you think Lucifer controlled the other cats?

a) Obviously he didn't, Elizabeth just thought he did.

b) The other cats just copied what he was doing.

c) Lucifer was giving them telepathic commands.

Q: How did the steak disappear from the oven?

a) Somebody stole it, knowing it would get blamed on the cats.

b) The cats pulled at the door together until it opened, then dragged away the steak and bashed the door shut behind them.

c) The cats apported the steak through the locked oven door.

Q: How did Anne learn to read?

a) By persevering.

b) She was helped by the friendly and comforting presence of Lucifer.

c) She received psychic energy from Lucifer.

Q: What happened when Elizabeth buried Lucifer?

a) She thought she saw a cat in the shadows.

b) She sensed the cat's spirit leaving its earthly home.

c) She saw the cat's spirit and heard it speak.

ASTROLOGY
FOR PETS

A psychic astrologer, Philip Solomon, believes that all pets and other animals, just like human beings, are influenced by the stars.

Philip has kindly prepared a sun-sign chart that will help you to decide if your pet is a real show-off Leo the Lion or a gentle and kindly Libra pet.

All you have to do is determine in which sign of the zodiac the sun was when your pet was born. You don't need a telescope, just follow the steps below.

Pet's birthday

1)   Check with your pet's papers or its breeder to discover the exact date of its birth.

2)   Refer to the zodiac table below and check the box next to the period in which your pet was born.

3)   Having discovered which sign your pet is, refer to the sun-sign chart.

4)   Enter your pet's name on the astrological certificate and compare its characteristics with those given as typical for its sign.

Birthday unknown?

If no one knows exactly when your pet was born, you can read the sun-sign chart first, then fill in the certificate and assign it a birthday based on its characteristics. It may not be the right day but at least you can celebrate.

ZODIAC TABLE		
December 21 to January 20	Capricorn	☐
January 20 to February 19	Aquarius	☐
February 19 to March 21	Pisces	☐
March 21 to April 19	Aries	☐
April 19 to May 20	Taurus	☐
May 20 to June 21	Gemini	☐
June 21 to July 22	Cancer	☐
July 22 to August 22	Leo	☐
August 22 to September 23	Virgo	☐
September 23 to October 23	Libra	☐
October 23 to November 21	Scorpio	☐
December 21 to January 20	Sagittarius	☐

SUN-SIGN CHART: PET

CAPRICORN:
Moody pets, but usually very friendly and steady most of the time. Capricorn pets may need more discipline and training than most other signs.

AQUARIUS:
Less emotional than many signs, the pet born under Aquarius can be very self-confident and rather aloof. They almost seem to able to speak and know their own minds and what they want.

PISCES:
Happy-go-lucky are pets born under Pisces. They seem to have not a care in the world and will befriend anyone. Cute, lovable pets but not great guard dogs.

ARIES:
Very strong-minded pets are often born under Aries. They like to show that they are number one. If an Aries pet loves you, you have a friend for life. A very loyal sign.

TAURUS:
Very possessive pets are usually born under Taurus. They want your love and attention all the time. Often quite stubborn and can be a bit greedy.

GEMINI:
Pets born under Gemini are very changeable. One day they love you to bits, the next they couldn't care less. Often very cunning, Gemini pets know how to get what they want.

CHARACTERISTICS

CANCER:

Home-loving pets are often Cancerians. They are very protective of those they love and make great house pets. You can love and trust a Cancer-sign pet and it will love you back.

LEO:

Impressive, confident and rather too proud for their own good. Leo pets are the kings of the pet world, or so they think. If you don't shower your Leo pets with love, they will sulk.

VIRGO:

Very choosy pets are born under Virgo. They tend to be one-person pets: they will love with all their might, but usually just the one very lucky individual. Can be a bit moody at times.

LIBRA:

Loving and friendly are Libra pets. They are easy-going, like peace and quiet and are very kind. They love good food and a nice clean bed. Pamper a Libra pet and you have a friend for life.

SCORPIO:

Pets with mysterious and very powerful personalities are born under Scorpio. They probably have the strongest characters of all the signs. They can love with a passion, but do not ever get them mad, they can have a bad temper.

SAGITTARIUS:

Very clever pets are those born under Sagittarius. Smart as a whip and able to get their owners to do almost anything for them. They love freedom but love their owners more. Sagittarian pets are lots of fun.

PET'S ASTROLOGICAL CERTIFICATE

Name of pet

_____

Breed

_____

Date of birth: day _____month _____ year_____

Sun sign _____

Main characteristics of my pet:

very affectionate ☐

friendly ☐

happy-go-lucky ☐

easy-going ☐

lots of fun ☐

strong personality ☐

likes to be spoiled ☐

likes freedom ☐

likes peace and quiet ☐

loves everyone ☐

loves only me ☐

protective ☐

possessive ☐

strong-minded ☐

knows what it wants ☐

choosy ☐

stubborn ☐

cunning ☐

manipulative ☐

needs training ☐

moody ☐

cool and aloof ☐

proud ☐

bad temper ☐

sulks ☐

clever ☐

loyal ☐

steady ☐

likes good food ☐

greedy ☐

clean ☐

changeable ☐

mysterious ☐

I have checked my pets characteristics and they are:

☐   typical of their sun sign

☐   typical of another sun sign

If so, which?

_____

THE HALLOWEEN CAT

October 31 is Halloween, the night when, according to tradition, ghosts and spirits walk the land. Certainly they believe this in and around the supposedly haunted hill called Eggardon.

The cat from the haunted hill

Anne Gurini was out alone that night in 1977 driving her car along a back country road between two tiny towns. In the moonlight, Eggardon hill rose darkly against the sky. Suddenly a deeper darkness descended as a cloud obscured the moon. Just then, in her headlights, Anne saw a black cat.

Thinking there was something wrong with it, she stopped her car and climbed out. The cat was crouching by the roadside, its jet-black fur glistening wet from the hilltop's marsh grass. The little creature cried, a thin, weak sound, as if it were close to death. Anne reached out, picked up the cat and snuggled it close to her chest.

A spooky paw

That night the strange cat slept quietly in Mrs. Gurini's den. She had given it fresh milk and a nibble of fish, then placed it under warm woolen blankets to await the day.

At the vet's the next morning, the surgeon examined Anne's foundling cat and considered it had been badly injured. He thought it might have been knocked down by a car and climbed up Eggardon hill to die. There Mrs. Gurini had found it as she drove home on Halloween.

The really weird thing the vet noticed was the cat had six claws on each paw, rather than five.

The cats conspire

Back at home Anne Gurini gave the black cat all the love and care she could. She named her Cheddar, to go with Anne's own cat Biscuit. Cheddar soon settled in, but there was something not quite right about her. She wouldn't let you stroke her and, as Anne looks back on events, she recalls that Cheddar seemed always to be aloof and self-important. Anne remembers thinking Cheddar was using her, watching her, as though she were waiting for something.

Anne was sure Biscuit and Cheddar liked each other. They seemed to have become close. Over the weeks Cheddar became much stronger. She would often go for walks around the house, and Biscuit always followed her.

But since Cheddar came into the house, Biscuit had changed. No longer was he quite so friendly; it was as though half his love belonged to Cheddar. He didn't snuggle up on Anne's knee any more. Now he just sat next to Cheddar and stared at her in a way that made Anne feel rather uneasy. It was as if the two cats knew something she didn't.

Getting her camera, Anne waited until the cats were seated together. She wanted some photographs of them side by side. She was going to show them to her friend who knew about weird things like spooks and hauntings. She had often told Anne that cats were supernatural creatures but Anne had just laughed the idea off. Now, as she watched the six-clawed Cheddar with her tabby cat Biscuit, she was not so sure.

A double vanishing

When Anne moved in the spring of 1978, Cheddar went missing. One night she just disappeared.

Some weeks later, Anne began to notice that Biscuit was behaving oddly. At night he would sit staring out of the window at the distant moon. It was as if he were waiting for something or someone.

Within a few days, Biscuit too was gone. Just like Cheddar before him, he left in the still of one dark night. Now both cats had vanished without trace.

More than a month had passed since Cheddar leaving home when Anne decided to have the film she had taken of the two cats developed. She was determined to show the pictures to her friend and ask if she could sense anything strange about the black cat she had found on that haunted hill on the night of Halloween.

When the film came back from the processing laboratory, the photographs that should have shown Cheddar were totally blank.

When Anne Gurini saw this, her blood ran cold. She believes that Cheddar was not a real cat but a spirit or witch cat from the world beyond. Anne thinks she came to collect her pet cat Biscuit as a friend and take him away with her into another supernatural place, perhaps even on haunted Eggardon hill.

When I spoke to Mrs. Gurini, she assured me that never again would she go near Eggardon hill at night, be it Halloween or any other day of the year. She has never seen or heard of either cat since.

PSYCHIC ASSESSMENT

Q: Why do you think the pictures of Cheddar failed to turn out?

a) Anne Gurini probably didn't take the lens cap off.

b) The film might have been faulty.

c) The cat was really a spirit that could not be photographed.

Q: Do you believe that Biscuit ran away to join Cheddar?

a) Cats are always running off; Biscuit could have gone anywhere.

b) Biscuit was lonely without his friend and went off to look for Cheddar.

c) Cheddar had put Biscuit under a kind of spell. After she had left, she returned to collect her friend.

THE AMAZING HOMING DOG

Pepsi is a Border collie–lurcher crossbreed who has baffled scientists with her ability to find her way home. Clive Rudkin, Pepsi's owner, who works as a nurse in an infirmary, bought her as a puppy in 1987 from the pound.

Pepsi's first escapade

It was when Pepsi escaped in the winter of 1990 that Clive first became aware of the dog's ability to find familiar places. Pepsi had somehow jumped the high garden wall at the back of his house and run off.

Clive was really upset. He couldn't sleep for wondering where Pepsi was. Then, after three days, the telephone rang. It was the pound. They said that Pepsi had been found outside their center, the place where she had been as a puppy. The worker had read the tag on Pepsi's collar and was calling to ask Clive to come and get her.

Happy again, Clive went straight over and brought his pet home.

An impromptu visit

Clive has many friends and relatives and often takes Pepsi with him when he goes to visit them. When out on her own, Pepsi seems able to find the homes of Clive's family and friends, despite only having been there once or twice. The strange thing is that she has usually been taken there by car—how does she find it on foot?

This amazing ability was demonstrated one summer afternoon when Pepsi and Clive were visiting his mother. Left in the back garden, Pepsi escaped and was missing for over four hours. Clive was very worried again, because his parents live in the middle of a large neighborhood surrounded by busy roads. He thought Pepsi might be hit by a car.

Then, for no clear reason, Clive suddenly thought he should phone his friend Jim to ask if he had seen the dog. When Jim answered the phone, he asked Clive to wait a second as there was a strange banging and knocking at the door. When Jim opened it, he saw Pepsi standing there.

Now Jim lives many miles away from Clive's parents and the journey between the houses would involve crossing main roads, parks, a river and numerous back streets. Only someone who knew exactly where they were going could make such a journey.

Pepsi had visited Jim's house on only one occasion, and then she had been taken there by Clive in his friend's car, so the dog could not have followed any scent. Neither could she have been following any landmarks known to her, for they had driven to Jim's from a different place. Clive was totally puzzled by just how Pepsi had found his friend's home, and why she had felt compelled to go there. But he was delighted she was safe.

Clive calls in the scientists

Over the years Pepsi has repeated her amazing escape and find-a-friend's-house trick many times. Once she even climbed out of Clive's bedroom window, jumped fourteen feet to the street below and ran off across town to Clive's parents' house.

This inexplicable ability so astounded Clive that he contacted Professor Rupert Sheldrake, an eminent biologist, who was conducting a series of experiments into psychic pets. Professor Sheldrake asked Clive if he might scientifically test Pepsi, using a special electronic transmitter linked to a satellite.

A television crew was invited to film this experiment for a TV series called *Out of This World*. Professor Sheldrake explained that the experiment was designed to test the dog's homing powers.

In the test, Pepsi was taken at four in the morning to an area, about two miles west of Clive's home. Professor Sheldrake tied the transmitter to Pepsi's back, the TV camera crew filmed and off she went.

Despite having to find her way from a totally unfamiliar area, in a very short space of time, Pepsi had arrived back home. She had a trot around the outside of the house and then, obviously enjoying her freedom, set out for more adventures.

As Pepsi traveled, the transmitter on her back beamed her location up to the satellite in the sky. This information, which gave the map coordinates of Pepsi, was relayed to Professor Sheldrake so that he could see exactly where she had been.

Pepsi crossed a number of urban streets, had a walk round the grounds of a local hospital and ended up in the back garden of Clive's sister's house, where she began eating grass. The distance she had traveled was over five miles.

Professor Sheldrake was unable to offer any logical explanation for Pepsi's behavior and ability. He did state that it was his belief that the dog may be tuning in to "morphic fields" (a concept he has put forward to explain a number of phenomena) and using these as a kind of homing signal to locate friendly places. In other words, the professor thought Pepsi had psychic powers.

Pepsi still escapes from time to time. She becomes restless and just decides to run off. But she can always find her way home. So if you happen to see Pepsi on the loose, don't worry: she knows where she's going.

PSYCHIC ASSESSMENT

Q: Why did Clive phone Jim when Pepsi ran away from his parents' house?

a) He was probably ringing everyone and started at Jim's.

b) He remembered that Jim had given Pepsi a treat when they visited.

c) Clive received a telepathic message from Pepsi.

Q: How does Pepsi find her way through the city streets to friendly houses?

a) She wanders about until she picks up a known scent.

b) She recognizes the houses and the area they are in, having been there before.

c) Pepsi has a special psychic power that tunes in to these homes.

TILLEY AND BUD: A FRIEND FROM BEYOND THE GRAVE

Bud was a big strong Rottweiler dog, all muscles and jaws. He looked really fierce. But inside this huge creature there was a soft heart. Bud even loved cats, at least his two Burmese housemates, Tilley and Harriet.

When they played together, Bud was extremely gentle with the cats and never hurt them. Tilley was Bud's favorite playmate; she would cuddle up to the Rottweiler and snuggle underneath his great chest. Often their owners, Joyce and Bill Nicholls would find all three curled up in a heap fast asleep.

Just before Christmas 1995 Bud became ill. He was not an old dog, only ten, but he died, and for weeks the family mourned the loss of their friend.

Tilley starts seeing things

About a month later, Joyce and her husband started to notice Tilley staring hard at the empty ceiling. Neither Joyce nor Bill could see anything there and Harriet, the other cat, seemed unaware of anything unusual. But Tilley could see something. Her eyes seemed to follow an unseen thing moving across the room.

Even Joyce's friends, who called to visit, would comment on the strange behavior of Tilley the cat. She would be sitting quite still, then suddenly look up as though disturbed by an unseen being, her eyes looking into vacant space.

Early one morning, as Bill was leaving for work, he saw Tilley walking about the front room as though following something. She had often walked alongside Bud in the same way.

Bill noticed a look of contentment on Tilley's little face, as though she were with a friend. Then he watched in amazement as she lay down in the corner of the room, in exactly the spot where Bud used to sleep. She seemed to be cuddling up to something and made a friendly mewing sound, just as she had when playing with the Rottweiler.

The hair on Bill's head almost stood on end, for he was sure that the cat was seeing the ghost of Bud. Yet Tilley was not afraid; she seemed to be enjoying herself.

Since she lost her friend Bud, Tilley's behavior has gone through changes. At first she obviously missed the Rottweiler, but now she seems quite happy playing with her invisible

companion. Whoever or whatever it might be.

Joyce likes to think that Bud returns now and again from the spirit world to say hello to his old friends, the two Burmese cats. It is only Tilley, though, that actually "sees" anything. Perhaps Tilley the cat now has a friend from beyond the grave.

PSYCHIC ASSESSMENT

Q: Why would Bud the Rottweiler want a cat as a friend?

a)   Bud was a big softy.

b)   Living in the same house with the cats, he learned to get on with them. A Rottweiler has nothing to prove.

c)   Bud and Tilley were on the same psychic wavelength.

Q: Do you believe that Bud returned from the grave?

a)   No, Tilley was probably looking at shadows or little flies.

b)   All cats have fits of staring into space. Who knows what they see?

c)   Yes, Tilley's actions were the same as when she had played with Bud. The cat could see the Rottweiler's ghost.

YOUR PSYCHIC PERSONALITY ASSESSMENT

Mostly As:

You're a cynic, a sceptic or a scientific materialist. Or else your pet is a stick insect.

You own an anorak, talk back to the teachers, and can't sing. Your favorite color is blue and your favorite computer game is Sim City. You understand odds and probability, and plan a career in science or finance.

Mostly Bs:

You have an open mind and hope one day your pet will reveal amazing powers, but it hasn't even learned to fetch yet.

You like long walks and lazy afternoons and have lots of friends. Once you had guitar lessons. Your favorite color is red. You read your horoscope in magazines but never remember to check whether it turned out to be right. You hope there will still be jobs when you grow up.

Mostly Cs:

You have a pig that can fly.

Your favorite color is purple, your favorite computer game is Myst, and you like to read about dragons. You play the guitar and are good at art. You'd like a job that involves lots of travel. Sometimes you watch the sunset on your own. You can instinctively tell if someone's a Scorpio.

Look out—what's that behind you?

BETTER THAN A

Lemonade $tand!

SMALL BUSINESS IDEAS
FOR
KIDS

by FIFTEEN-YEAR-OLD Daryl Bernstein

illustrations by ROB HUSBERG

WANT TO EARN YOUR OWN MONEY?
LEARN HOW TO START A BUSINESS!

15-year-old Daryl Bernstein started his first business when he was just eight-years-old. Since then he's tried all 51 of the businesses in the book. Daryl now runs his own multi-million dollar business and is ready to share his secrets with you!

Learn fun ways to earn $$$ as a ...
Babysitting Broker
Dog Walker
Mural Painter
Snack Vendor

... and many, many more!!!

"Dear Daryl,
When I got 'Better Than A Lemonade Stand,' I came up with a great business idea and earned enough money to buy a laptop computer! I've wanted my own computer for a long time. I never knew it would only take one summer to earn the money. Thanks for your help."
—Brady, age 12

Business, 150 pages, black & white cartoon illustrations, $8.95 softcover, $14.95 hardcover

For a free catalog or to order books,
call Beyond Words Publishing 1-800-284-9673

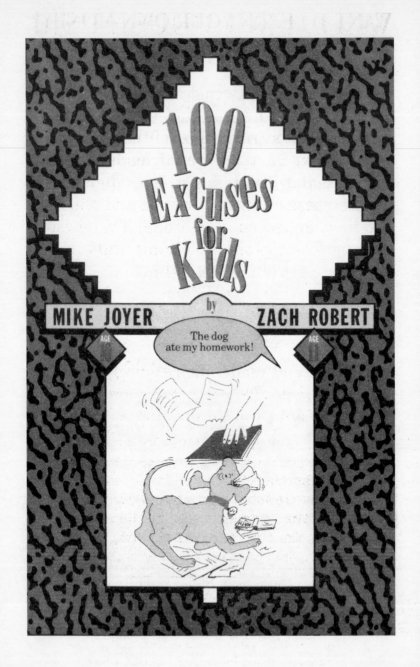

WELL, EXCUUUUSE US!!!

HERE ARE ALL THE EXCUSES YOU'LL EVER NEED!

Mike and Zach are the excuse experts! At ages 10 and 11, these best friends came up with this very funny book idea. They tested their excuses on family, friends and teachers and have appeared on national TV, newspapers and magazines, giving kids great excuses to get out of everything.

You'll get the best excuses for ...
going to bed late
not eating your vegetables
getting your allowance raised
not cleaning your room
... and many, many more!!!

> "Dear Mike and Zach,
> My whole class loves your book! I have an idea for excuses not to do your homework in the car: 'But Mom, it's homework, not carwork!' —Blakeney, age 10

Humor, 96 pages, black & white cartoon illustrations, $5.95 softcover

For a free catalog or to order books,
call Beyond Words Publishing 1-800-284-9673

HEY, GIRLS!!!

SPEAK OUT
BE HEARD
BE CREATIVE
GO FOR YOUR
DREAMS

Girls Know Best celebrates your unique voices and wisdom. 38 girls, ages 7-15, were picked to share their advice and activities with other girls. Everything you need to know... from the people who really know the answers—girls just like you!

Discover how you can ...

handle grouchy, just plain ornery adults
pass notes in class without getting caught
avoid life's most embarrassing moments
make home-made beauty recipes
unlock the writer inside you
... and much, much more!!!

Advice/Activity, 160 pages, black & white
illustrations, $8.95 softcover

HOW ARE YOU GOING TO ROCK THE WORLD?

Girls Who Rocked the World is a collection of 35 girls who did amazing things and changed the world before they even turned 20-years-old! These incredible girls will show you what can happen when you believe in yourself and in "girl power!"

Learn about girls who rocked the world, like:

＊ Joan of Arc was just 17 when she led French armies into battles against the English.

＊ Phillis Wheatley was a slave from Africa, but at 17 she became a published poet.

＊ Cristen Powell was 16 when she became the youngest female drag race winner in history.

Biography, 112 pages, black & white illustrations, $8.95 softcover

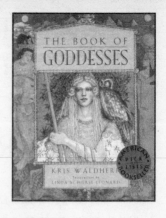